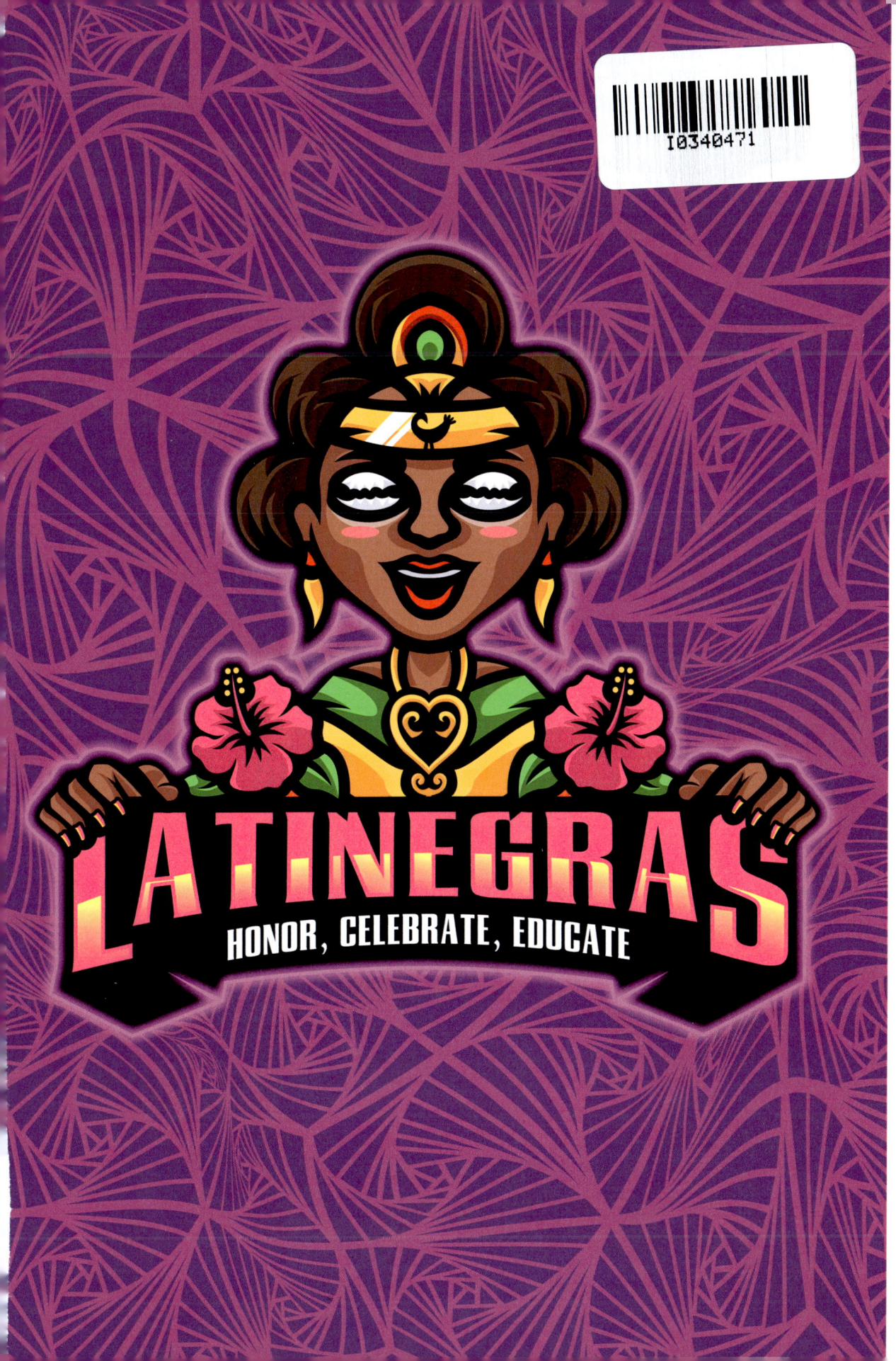

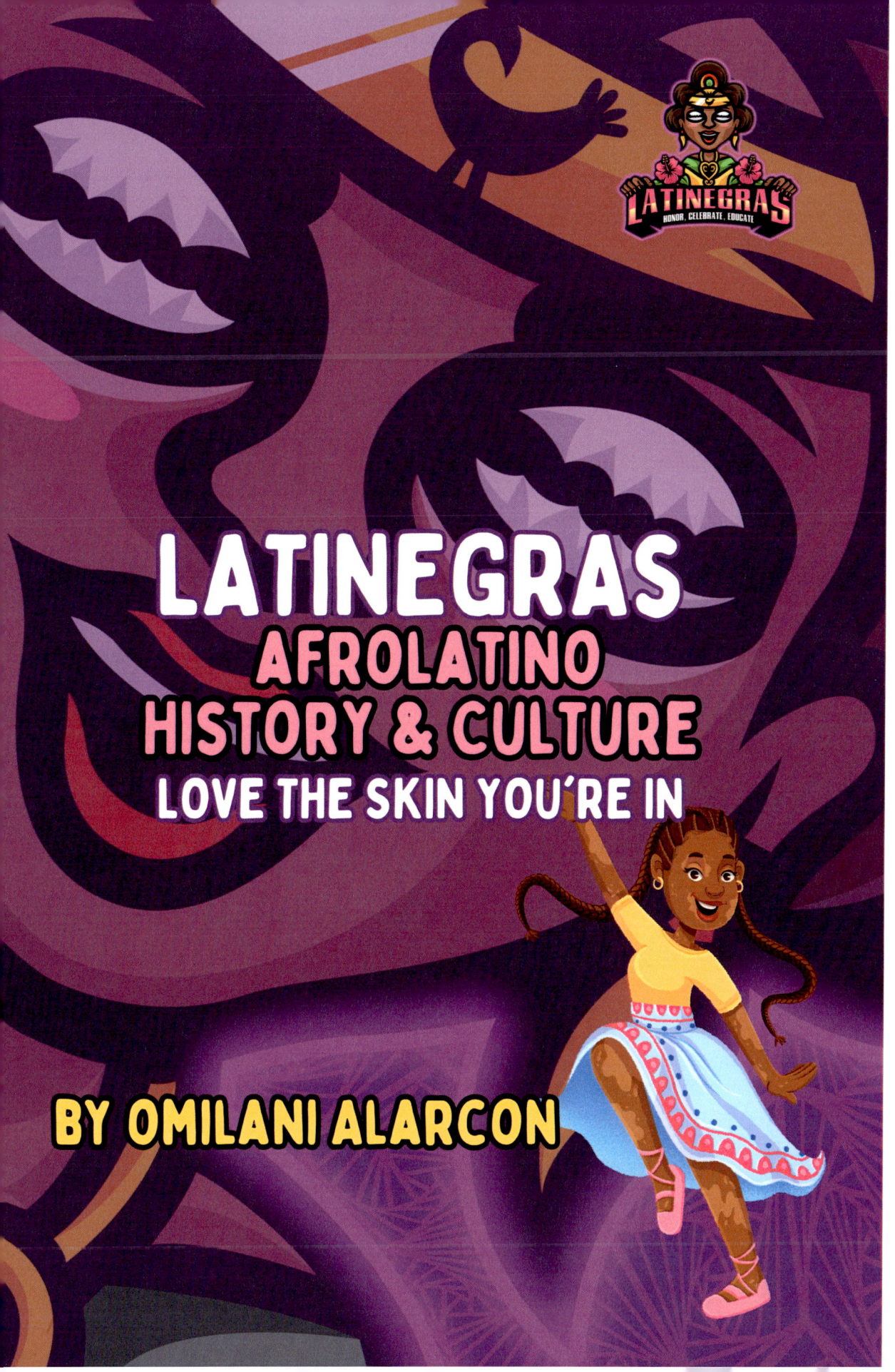

FOREWORD

MY PARENTS ARE EDUCATORS WITH MY MOTHER BEING AN ENGLISH TEACHER AND MY DAD A HISTORIAN. FROM A YOUNG AGE MY CURIOSITY WAS FUELED FOR ALL THINGS ACADEMIC.

MY PARENTS KEPT THE MOST EXTENSIVE LIBRARY IN THE HOUSE AND BOOKS INTERESTED ME FAR MORE THAN DOLLS AND PLAY HOUSES. I REMEMBER IMMERSING MYSELF IN BOOKS SUCH AS "BEFORE THE MAYFLOWER" AND ANTHOLOGIES OF POETRY FROM LITERARY GREATS LIKE LANGSTON HUGHES AND COUNTEE CULLEN. HOWEVER, IT WAS J.A. ROGERS' "100 AMAZING FACTS ABOUT [BLACK PEOPLE]" THAT REALLY CAPTIVATED MY INTEREST. EACH PAGE WAS LIKE A TREASURE TROVE OF JUICY HISTORY, INVENTIONS, AND MIND-BOGGLING FACTS THAT KEPT ME HOOKED.

LATINEGRAS: AFROLATINO HISTORY & CULTURE AIMS TO BE A FUN AND INTERACTIVE EXPLOSION OF HISTORICAL TIDBITS, JUST LIKE ROGERS' MASTERPIECE. IT IS AN INTRODUCTION TO THE WONDERFUL WORLD OF AFRO-LATINO HISTORY, PACKED WITH JUICY NUGGETS OF INFORMATION WITHOUT BEING TOO HEAVY. THIS IS JUST THE FIRST OF A SERIES OF BOOKS I HOPE TO COMPLETE THAT REFLECT THE TYPE OF BOOK I WISH I HAD GROWING UP. IT WAS NOT EASY NAVIGATING THE WORLD AS A LATINEGRA AND AFROFILIPINA CHILD. AT TIMES IT WAS EVEN PAINFUL. I WRITE SO THE NEXT GENERATION WILL NOT HAVE THE SAME STRUGGLES AS I HAVE ENDURED.

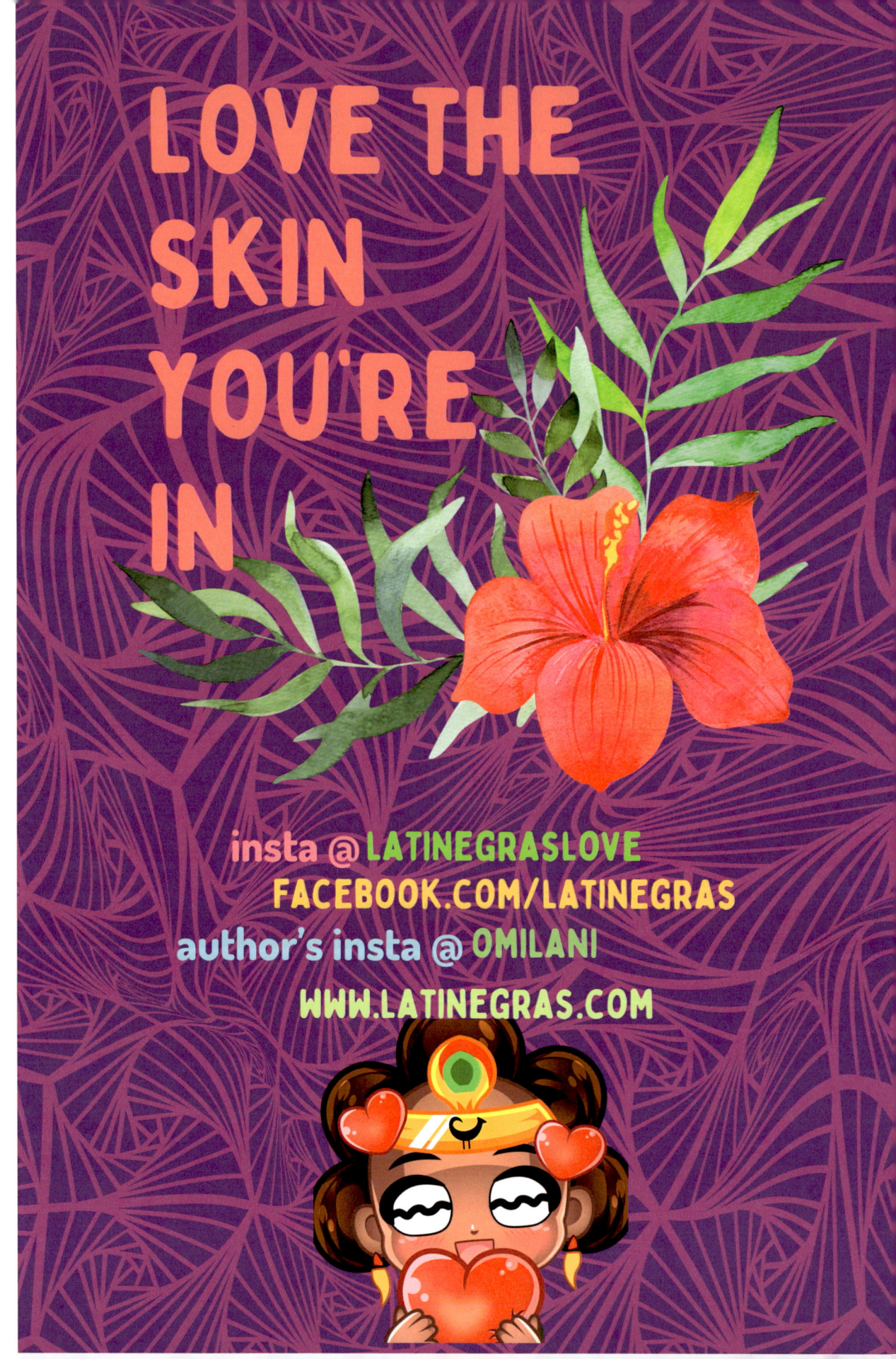

TABLE OF CONTENTS

1. FOREWORD
2. LATINEGRAS
3. HISTORY
   A. MOORS
   B. ENSLAVEMENT
   C. HAITIAN REVOLUTION
   D. MAROONS
   E. DIASPORA
   F. SPANISH WORDS AFRICAN ORIGIN
4. NOTABLE AFROLATINOS
5. LATINEGRAS SONG
6. LATINEGRAS FILM
   A. HOW IT STARTED
   B. CAST MEMBERS
   C. THROUGH THE YEARS
7. MEANING BEHIND LATINEGRAS LOGO

APETEBI

OMILANI - FROM ALBUM ORE YEYE O

RIGHT NOW I CARRY WITH ME
THE STORY OF 1,000 CENTURIES
THAT SPANS FROM AFRICA TO THE PACIFIC SEAS

I'M YORUBA AND I'M CONGO
ZAMBOANGA AND ILONGGO
THE JOURNEY OF A MILLION ISLES LIVES WITH ME

I'M JUST AN ISLAND GIRL
LIVING IN A MODERNIZED WORLD
TRYING TO FULFILL MY DESTINY - APETEBI

BORN A DIVINER 'CAUSE I SEE RIGHT THROUGH
BORN A SURVIVOR
ANCESTORS CAME THROUGH
SUGARCANE VEINS
I'M A CAROLINA BELL
RIDING ON A STINGRAY
I'M A FILIPINA GIRL

I'M BOMBA AND TAINO
SWEET PLANTAIN MOFONGO
ON A JEEPNEY FROM MANILA
SPEAKING CHAVACANO
PROPELLED BY A PAST THAT PREPARES ME
FOR MY FUTURE
I'M THAT MINDANAO SOLDIER
AND A PRIEST FROM ABEOKUTA

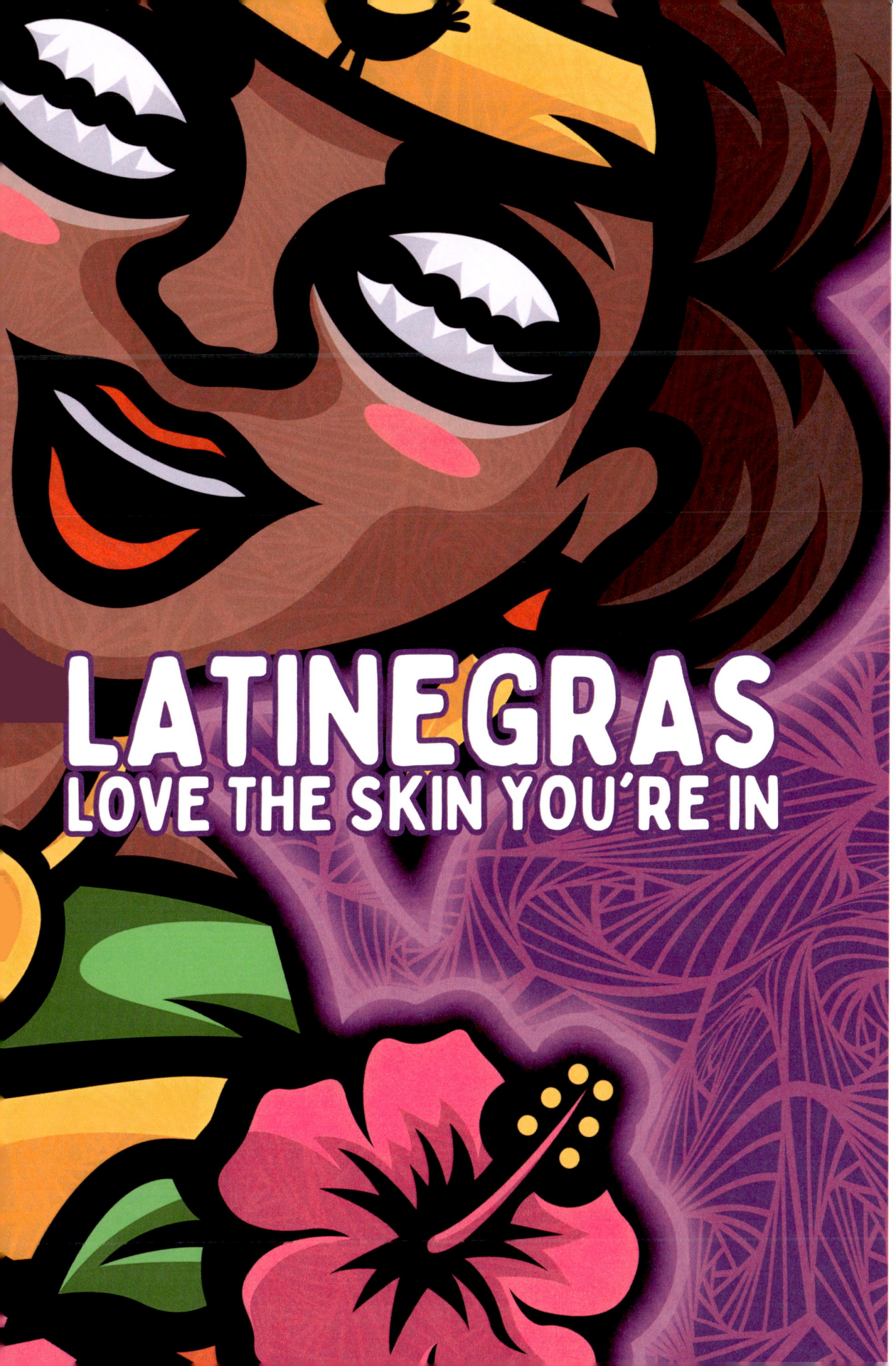

LATINEGRAS

ORIGINAL POEM

CURLY HAIR AND A BROWN FACE TO MATCH
I WASN'T ALWAYS PROUD OF THAT
I WAS TOLD A LATINA AIN'T BLACK
SO STOP WITH THAT
BUT WHEN I WALKED OUT ON THE STREET
WHAT DID I SEE?

MORENITAS JUST LIKE ME
SO I LEARNED TO LOVE ME
CAUSE I CAN'T CHANGE IT
STEPPIN' OUT WITH DIGNITY
THE WAY GOD MADE ME
LATINEGRA, COMO SOY YO
DE LA ISLA NUEVA YORK

SOY AJENA - NUYORICAN
CASI GRINGA - AMER-REE-KIN

LATINEGRA JUST LIKE ME
MORENITA - COLORFUL ME
I DIDN'T FIT IN
WITH MY BROWN SKIN
CASI GRINGA
AMER-REE-CAN

WHAT IS LATINEGRA

LATINEGRA IS ANOTHER WAY OF SAYING AFROLATINA IT MEANS YOU HAVE AFRICAN ANCESTRY AND ROOTS IN LATIN AMERICA.

NOT ALL LATINEGRAS OR LATINEGROS SPEAK SPANISH OR WERE BORN IN LATIN AMERICA. IN FACT, THERE ARE MANY PEOPLE BORN AND RAISED IN LATIN AMERICA THAT DO NOT SPEAK SPANISH. THERE ARE MANY INDIGENOUS LANGUAGES, INCLUDING SOME THAT ARE PRIMARILY SPOKEN BY AFROLATINOS LIKE THE GARIFUNA LANGUAGE.

ALWAYS REMEMBER YOU ARE ENOUGH!

YOU DON'T HAVE TO SHOW PICTURES OF YOUR "LATINO" LOOKING FAMILY MEMBERS OR LIKE SALSA MUSIC OR EVEN LIKE TO EAT LATINO FOOD TO BE LATINA.

SOMETIMES WE DON'T EVEN KNOW OUR FULL FAMILY HISTORY AND THAT'S OK TOO! IT IS NOT YOUR FAULT AND YOU ARE STILL **ENOUGH**

LATINEGRA IS A COMBINATION OF TWO WORDS.

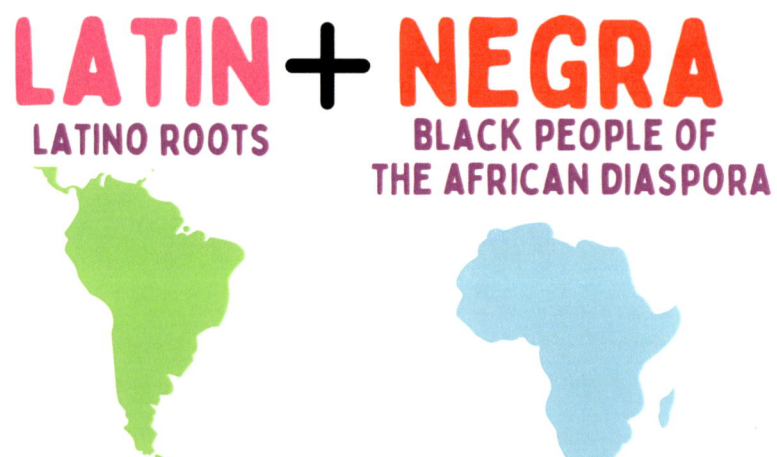

THE EARLIEST RECORDING OF IT BEING USED WAS IN THE 1970'S BY XEÑON CRUZ, AND THEN LATER ON BY PSYCHOLOGIST DR. LILLIAN COMAS DIAZ.

AFROLATINOS LOOK SO MANY DIFFERENT WAYS. SOME HAVE BEAUTIFUL CURLY HAIR OR GORGEOUS AFRO HAIR. SOME HAVE STRAIGHT HAIR, WAVY HAIR OR EVEN NO HAIR AT ALL!

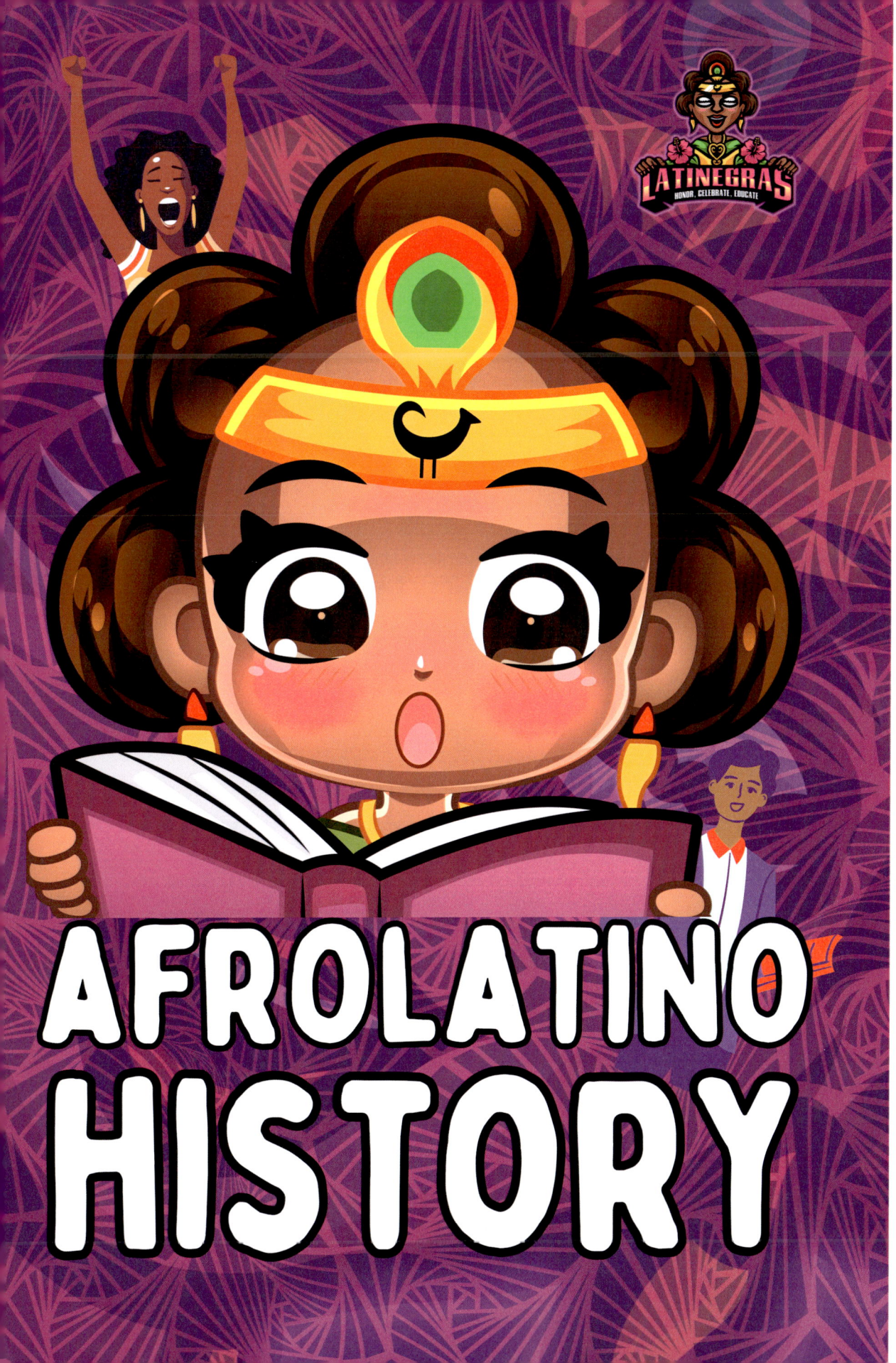

HISTORY

OUR HISTORY DOES NOT START WITH SLAVERY/ENSLAVEMENT. OUR HISTORY BEGINS IN AFRICA LONG BEFORE COLONIZERS INVADED THE LANDS. EVERY KIND OF PERSON YOU CAN IMAGINE EXISTED IN AFRICA. THERE WERE SCIENTISTS AND MERCHANTS, MATHEMATICIANS AND FARMERS. THERE WERE GREAT SCHOOLS AND FAMOUS SCHOLARS LIKE IMHOTEP.

SOME WERE WARRIORS AND ROYALS WHILE OTHERS WERE TEACHERS, HEALERS AND TRADITIONAL PRIESTS AMONG MANY OTHER PROFESSIONS.

THERE WERE GREAT CITIES IN AFRICA AND MAJOR CIVILIZATIONS. SOME OF THE MOST FAMOUS ARE ANCIENCT NUBIA (EGYPT), TIMBUKTU (MALI), AND THE OYO EMPIRE (NIGERIA).

MOORS

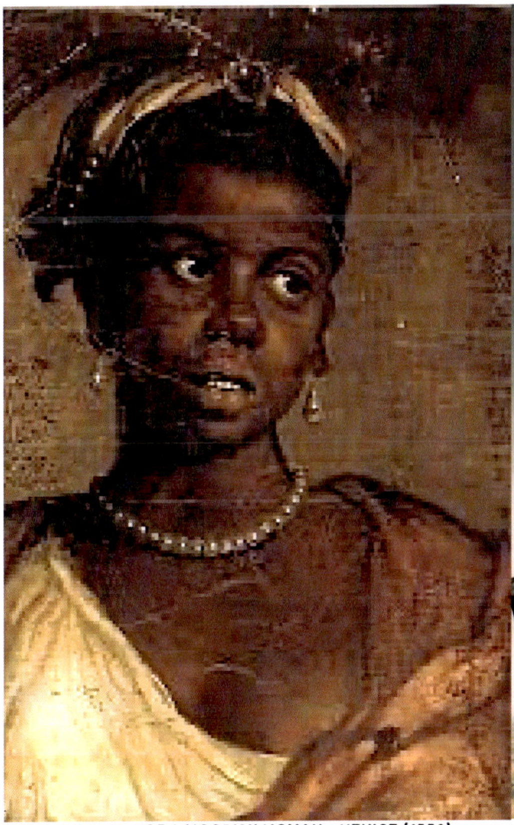

PORTRAIT OF A MOORISH WOMAN - VENICE (1550)

AFRICAN MOORS RULED SPAIN FOR MORE THAN 500 YEARS AND THE MOORS BROUGHT LANGUAGE, TECHNOLOGY, EDUCATION AND HYGENE TO SOUTHERN EUROPE.

TARIQ BIN ZIYAD COMMANDED THE MOORISH ARMY THAT DEFEATED THE VISIGOTHS IN SOUTHERN SPAIN AT THE ROCK OF GIBRALTAR AROUND APRIL 26, 711 AD.

AS A MATTER OF FACT, SOME SAY THE ROCK OF GIBRALTAR IS NAMED AFTER HIM, JABAL TARIQ.

THE INFLUENCE OF THE MOORS IS SIGNIFICANT AND THEY WERE ADVANCED IN SO MANY WAYS.

THE MOORS CARRIED NEW PLANTS LIKE ORANGES, POMEGRANATES, SILK, RICE, AND FIGS.

THEY BROUGHT ARCHITECHETURE, PLUMBING SYSTEMS AND HYGIENE. THE MOORS WERE VERY CLEAN.

ALSO, EDUCATION WAS EXTREMELY IMPORTANT TO THEM AND THEY SPREAD LITERACY AND OTHER FORMS OF EDUCATION IN COMPARISON WITH THE 90% ILLITERACY THEY MET IN SOUTHERN EUROPE.

OUR CURRENT NUMERIC (1.2.3.) SYSTEM IS BASED ON THE ARABIC NUMBERS BROUGHT TO EUROPE BY THE MOORS AND REPLACED THE ROMAN NUMERALS.

DID YOU KNOW?

LATINEGRAS DEBUTED IN SEVILLE, ANDALUCIA SPAIN.

WE ATTENDED THE ASWAD (ASSOCIATION FOR THE STUDY OF THE WORLDWIDE AFRICAN DIASPORA) CONFERENCE AND PRESENTED A PAPER WITH ACTRESS/AUTHOR INDHIRA SERRANO AND SCREENED THE FILM LATINEGRAS TO A FULL AUDIENCE.

AFRICA WAS RICH WITH TECHNOLOGY, EDUCATION, SPIRITUALITY, LITERACY, NAVIGATION AND ALL TYPES OF ARCHITECTURE.

ENSLAVEMENT

THE INTELLIGENCE AND IMMENSE TECHNOLOGICAL ADVANCEMENT OF AFRICA IN PRECOLONIAL TIMES HAS BEEN WELL DOCUMENTED. IN WALTER RODNEY'S HOW EUROPE UNDERDEVELOPED AFRICA, HE TALKS ABOUT HOW COLONIALISM EXPLOITED AND INTENTIONALLY DECONSTRUCTED THE POWER AND TALENT OF AFRICA TO MAKE IT UNDERDEVELOPED. PART OF THIS UNDERDEVELOPMENT IS ENSLAVEMENT.

AFRICANS WERE KIDNAPPED AND STOLEN FROM AFRICA. THEY WERE TAKEN AWAY FROM THEIR FAMILES AND FRIENDS AND THE LIFE THEY KNEW BEFORE THE TRANS ATLANTIC SLAVE TRADE.

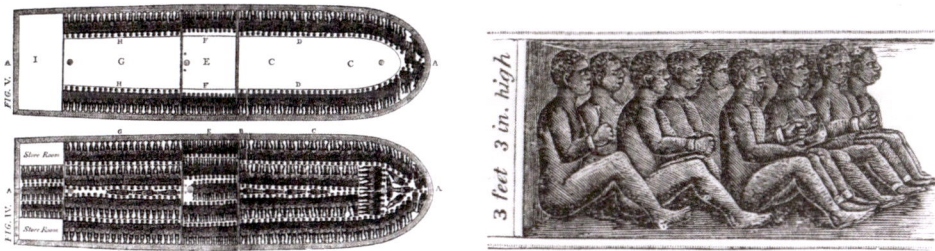

MANY WERE TAKEN FROM THE WEST COAST AND SOME FROM CENTRAL AFRICA.

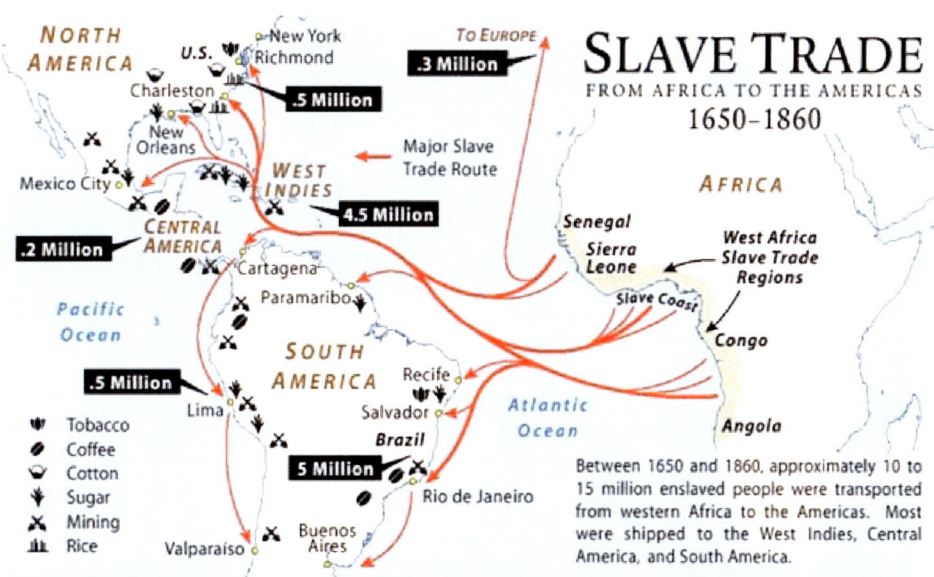

VIA MAP OF THE WEEK: SLAVE TRADE FROM AFRICA TO THE AMERICAS 1650-1860 - RICHMOND.EDU

MORE THAN 10 MILLION AFRICANS WERE DROPPED IN THE CARIBBEAN AND SOUTH AMERICA. OF THAT 10 MILLION, 500 THOUSAND WERE TAKEN TO THE UNITED STATES AND 350 THOUSAND WERE TAKEN TO EUROPE.

ENSLAVEMENT NOT ONLY DISPLACED MILLIONS OF PEOPLE AND DISCONNECTED THEM FROM THEIR HOMELANDS, IT ALSO CHANGED WHO THE PEOPLE WOULD BECOME FOREVER.

THEIR RELIGION, THEIR TRADITIONS, NAMES, AND EVEN THE INSTRUMENTS LIKE THE DRUMS WERE STRIPPED FROM THEM AND IN SOME CASES MADE ILLEGAL. THERE WAS A LOT OF EFFORT TO ERASE THESE IDENTITIES, YET, THROUGH THE RESILLIANCE OF AFRICAN PEOPLE, A LOT OF THE CULTURE AND IDENTITY SURVIVED.

SOMETIMES IT WAS HIDDEN OR MASKED TO PROTECT THE TRADITIONS WHILE APPEARING TO "ACCEPT" THE COLONIAL TRADITIONS THAT WERE IMPOSED UPON THEM.

FROM BEING KIDNAPPED TO COLONIZATION, AFRICA'S DESCENDANTS RESISTED IN SO MANY WAYS. SOME WERE LOST AT SEA WHILE OTHERS SURVIVED THE MIDDLE PASSAGE AND REVOLTED IN VARIOUS WAYS IN THE COLONIZED AMERICAS.

HAITIAN REVOLUTION

TOUSSAINT L'OUVERTURE   JEAN JACQUES DESSALINES

THE HAITIAN REVOLUTION WAS NOT AN **EVENT**. IT WAS A **TWELVE YEAR RESISTANCE** FROM 1791-1804. IT HAS BEEN RECORDED AS THE MOST SUCCESSFUL REVOLT OF ENSLAVED PEOPLE THEREBY MAKING SAINT DOMINGUE (HAITI) THE FIRST INDEPENDENT BLACK NATION IN THE AMERICAS.

TOUSSAINT L'OUVERTURE LED THE CHARGE OF SAINT DOMINGUE'S INDEPENDENCE FROM FRENCH COLONIAL RULE.

NAPOLEON BONAPARTE BRIEFLY REGAINED CONTROL OF HAITI IN 1802 AND IN 1804 JEAN JACQUES DESSALINES LED THE HAITIAN TROOPS WITH A DIFFERENT APPROACH. HE COMBINED MILLITARY INTELLIGENCE WITH THE AID OF AFRICAN DERIVED PRACTICES. THE STORY IS THAT A WOMAN WENT TO THE TOP OF THE MOUNTAIN AND GAVE A BLACK CREOLE PIG AS AN OFFERING FOR PROTECTION AND SUCCESS.

HAITI SUCCESSFULLY DEFEATED THE FRENCH BECOMING THE FIRST BLACK NATION IN THE AMERICAS TO SUCCESSFULLY REVOLT AND OVERTHROW COLONIAL RULE.

MAROONS

RESISTANCE MOVEMENTS CONTINUED THROUGHOUT THE AMERICAS AS **AFRICAN DESCENDANTS** SOUGHT **FREEDOM** AND **ESCAPE** FROM ENSLAVEMENT.

OF COURSE, WHEN PEOPLE SEE THE WORD MAROON, THEY MAY THINK OF THE COLOR. HOWEVER, THAT IS NOT THE FULL DEFINITION. THE WORD MAROON IS RECORDED AS BEING IN USE AS EARLY AS **1590** AND IS A DREIVATIVE FROM THE FRENCH WORD **MARRON** MEANING 'FERAL' OR "FUGITIVE". IN FACT, ACCORDING TO THE OXFORD DICTIONARY, THE COLOR **MARRON**, A REDDISH BROWN COLOR DID NOT APPEAR UNTIL THE LATE **1700S** AND MAY HAVE DERIVED FROM THE IDEA OF THERE BEING A **MARRON** PEOPLES.

IN SPANISH, THE WORD CIMMARON IS ALSO OFTEN GIVEN AS THE SOURCE OF THE ENGLISH WORD MAROON. IN THE EARLY 1570'S, SIR FRANCIS DRAKE'S RAIDS ON THE SPANISH IN PANAMA WERE AIDED BY "SYMERONS," A CREOLIZED VERSION OF THE WORD CIMARRÓN.

CUBAN PHILOLOGIST (A LINGUIST WHO FINDS CLUES IN LITERATURE) JOSÉ JUAN ARROM, THEORIZED THAT THE ARAWAK (INDIGENOUS) WORD SIMARABO PREDATED BOTH THE SPANISH CIMARRÓN AND THE ENGLISH DERIVATIVE MAROON. ACCORDING TO ARROM, IT WAS FIRST USED IN HISPANIOLA IN REFERENCE TO WILD CATTLE, THEN TO THE ENSLAVED INDIGENOUS WHO FLED TO THE HILLS, AND BY THE EARLY 1530'S IT WAS USED IN REFERENCE TO AFRICAN CAPTIVES WHO DID THE SAME. IN EACH CASE, THE WORD MAROON, MARRON OR CIMARRON ALL REFER TO WILD OR FUGITIVE HUMANS OR ANIMALS. IT IS UNFORTUNATE THAT MANY OF THE KIDNAPPED AND STOLEN AFRICAN PEOPLE WERE TREATED AS ANIMALS FROM THE TIME THEY WERE TAKEN FROM THEIR HOMES TO THE NEW WORLD.

MAROON COMMUNITIES EXISTED FROM NORTH AMERICA ALL THE WAY TO CENTRAL/SOUTH AMERICA,

MAROONS

TO THE CARIBBEAN AND EVEN TO ISLANDS IN THE INDIAN OCEAN. AFRICAN MAROONS INTERMIXED AND LIVED TOGETHER WITH INDIGENOUS COMMUNITIES. THEY FORMED THEIR OWN CREOLE LANGUAGES AND MANY FLED TO THE MOUNTAINS, HILLS, OR TERRAINS THAT FOR OTHERS WAS CONSIDERED VERY DANGEROUS TO NAVIGATE.

THE IDEA THAT AFRICAN PEOPLE ACCEPTED ENSLAVEMENT AND JUST COMPLACENTLY FELL INTO THE INHUMANE SYSTEM OF SLAVERY COULD NOT BE FURTHER FROM THE TRUTH. ESCAPE AND REBELLION IN THE NEW WORLD HAS BEEN DOCUMENTED AS EARLY AS 1512.

VENTA DE ESCLAVOS.

UNA NEGRA se vende, recien parida, con abundante leche, escelente lavandera y planchadora, con principios de cocina, jóven, sana y sin tachas, y muy humilde: darán razon en la calle de O Reilly n.º 16, el portero.   6 30

UNA NEGRA se vende por no necesitarla su dueño, de nacion conga, como de 20 años, con su cria de 11 meses, sana y sin tachas, muy fiel y humilde, no ha conocido mas amo que el actual, es regular lavandera, planchadora y cocinera: en la calle del Baratillo casa n.º 4 informarán.   31

VENTA DE ANIMALES.

SANGUIJUELAS de buen tamaño y sobresaliente calidad, se hallan de venta en la barbería plazuela de S. Juan de Dios, y tambien en la calle del Sol esquina á la de Compostela frente á la hojalatería, barbería de Reyes Satiesteban á peso doc.ª, con la satisfaccion que pueden devolver las que no peguen por casualidad, pues con lo que garantizo lo buenas que son, y puesta por el mismo autor con la velocidad de 2 minutos, como lo tiene acreditado con las principales familias de esta capital, por 12 rs. doc. bien sean fuertes ó sencillos.   30-4

VENTA DE LIBROS.

LOS HIJOS DEL TIO TRONERA.

PARODIA DEL TROVADOR. Este chistosísimo sainete picaresco, en verso, original del célebre poeta D. Antonio Garcia Gutierrez, y que fué tan aplaudido en el gran teatro de esta capital, se ha impreso con el mayor esmero, y se halla de venta á 2 rs. senc. en la librería de

THE STATUE OF "THE FREED SLAVE" IN MEMORIAL HALL.

Death of Capt. Ferrer, the Captain of the Amistad, July, 1839.

Don Jose Ruiz and Don Pedro Montez, of the Island of Cuba, having purchased fifty-three slaves at Havana, recently imported from Africa, put them on board the Amistad, Capt. Ferrer, in order to transport them to Principe, another port on the Island of Cuba. After being out from Havana about four days, the African captives on board, in order to obtain their freedom, and return to Africa, armed themselves with cane knives, and rose upon the Captain and crew of the vessel. Capt. Ferrer and the cook of the vessel were killed; two of the crew escaped; Ruiz and Montez were made prisoners.

SE HA HUIDO.

En la mañana del 25 del corriente un negrito llamado Joaquin, de edad como de 10 á 12 años; habla poco castellano, vá vestido con pantalon de paño azul y una camisa de color con ramitos morados; es muy alto y bastante renegrido. La persona que lo halle y quiera presentarlo en la barraca de D. Pablo Duplesis en la calle de san Benito número 30, será gratificada.

20.1.1840

MAROONS

THE **FIRST REVOLT** OF **AFRICANS** ENSLAVED IN THE AMERICAS TOOK PLACE IN **26 DECEMBER 1521** IN WHAT IS KNOWN AS THE PRESENT DAY **DOMINICAN REPUBLIC**.

SEBASTIÁN LEMBA, BORN IN **AFRICA**, **SUCCESSFULLY REBELLED** AGAINST THE SPANIARDS (IN THE DOMINICAN REPUBLIC) IN 1532, AND BANDED TOGETHER WITH **OTHER AFRICANS** IN HIS 15-YEAR STRUGGLE AGAINST THE SPANISH COLONISTS. MANY REBELLIONS THEREAFTER WERE **INSPIRED** BY SEBASTIÁN LEMBA.

SEBASTIÁN LEMBA

MAROONS

HERE ARE A FEW HIGHLIGHTS IN MAROON HISTORY IN LATIN AMERICA, THE CARIBBEAN AND THE AMERICAS.

QUEEN NANNY OF THE MAROONS

JAMAICA

QUEEN NANNY HAILED FROM THE ASHANTI TRIBE IN GHANA AND WAS BORN AROUND 1686. SHE AND THREE OF HER BROTHERS WERE CAPTURED AND SHIPPED TO JAMAICA. THEY FLED AND FOUND RETREAT IN THE BLUE MOUNTAINS. NANNY AROSE TO BECOME A FIERCE MILITARY LEADER WHO PROTECTED THE MAROON PEOPLE IN THE MOUNTAINS AND TRAINED THEM TO OUTSMART AND DEFEAT THE BRITISH. SHE IS STILL A NATIONAL HERO. NANNY TOWN WAS NAMED IN HER HONOR. LATER THE NAME CHANGED TO MOOR TOWN AND ALTHOUGH THE DETAILS OF HER DEATH ARE UNCERTAIN, A MEMORIAL GRAVE WAS BUILT IN HER HONOR. SHE WAS GIVEN THE TITLE, "RIGHT EXCELLENT," WHICH ONLY 7 NATIONAL FIGURES HOLD AND SHE IS THE ONLY WOMAN. SHE NOW APPEARS ON THE $500 JAMAICAN MONETARY NOTE.

MAROONS

FRANÇOIS MAKANDAL   HAITI

(1730-c. 1758) was a Haitian Maroon leader in the French colony of Saint-Domingue (present-day Haiti). He is described as a Haitian Vodou priest, or Houngan. It is known that he had an immense knowledge of plants and herbs that were used as poision to combat the French soldiers. He was also well-versed in Arabic and may be from the Mahgreb, Senegal, Mali or Guinea. He united with Maroons to kill slave owners in Saint-Domingue, his confidant was tortured and revealed secrets that led to his capture. Makandal was burned alive by French colonial authorities.

MAROONS

- **PANAMA** - BAYANO, A MANDINKA MAN WHO HAD BEEN ENSLAVED AND TAKEN TO PANAMA IN 1552, LED A REBELLION AGAINST THE SPANISH IN PANAMA. HE AND HIS FOLLOWERS ESCAPED TO FOUND VILLAGES IN THE LOWLANDS.
- **MEXICO** - GASPAR YANGA WAS AN AFRICAN LEADER OF A MAROON COLONY IN THE VERACRUZ HIGHLANDS IN WHAT IS NOW MEXICO. IT IS BELIEVED YANGA HAD BEEN A FUGITIVE SINCE THE EARLY 1570'S, AND WAS THE LEADER OF A FORMIDABLE GROUP OF MAROONS. IN 1609, YANGA NEGOTIATED WITH THE SPANISH COLONISTS TO ESTABLISH A SELF-RULED MAROON SETTLEMENT CALLED SAN LORENZO DE LOS NEGROS (LATER RENAMED YANGA).

YANGA WAS MEXICO'S FIRST OFFICIALLY RECOGNIZED MAROON CITY

Painting at Museo Regional de Palmillas, Yanga Veracruz via Wikimedia Commons

MAROONS

FLORIDA SEMINOLES

John Horse/Juan Caballo
Black Seminole War Leader

- FLORIDA - BLACK SEMINOLES - SEMINOLE INDIANS WERE ONE OF THE LARGEST AND MOST SUCCESSFUL MAROON COMMUNITIES IN FLORIDA DUE TO MORE RIGHTS AND FREEDOMS GRANTED BY THE SPANISH EMPIRE. SOME AFRODESCENDANTS INTERMARRIED AND WERE CULTURALLY SEMINOLE; OTHERS MAINTAINED A MORE AFRICAN CULTURE. DESCENDANTS OF THOSE WHO WERE DISPLACED WITH THE SEMINOLE TO INDIGENOUS TERRITORY IN THE 1830S ARE RECOGNIZED AS BLACK SEMINOLES.

- BRAZIL - PALMARES - ONE OF THE BEST-KNOWN QUILOMBOS (MAROON SETTLEMENTS) IN BRAZIL WAS PALMARES (THE PALM NATION), WHICH WAS FOUNDED IN THE EARLY 17TH CENTURY. AT ITS HEIGHT, IT HAD A POPULATION OF OVER 30,000 FREE PEOPLE AND WAS RULED BY KING ZUMBI. PALMARES MAINTAINED ITS INDEPENDENT EXISTENCE FOR ALMOST A HUNDRED YEARS UNTIL IT WAS CONQUERED BY THE PORTUGUESE IN 1694.

MAROONS

- **COLOMBIA** - **SANTA MARTA** - ESCAPED AFRODESCENDANTS ESTABLISHED INDEPENDENT COMMUNITIES ALONG THE REMOTE PACIFIC COAST, OUTSIDE OF THE REACH OF THE COLONIZERS. AT THE START OF THE SEVENTEENTH CENTURY, A GROUP OF RUNAWAYS HAD ESTABLISHED A PALENQUE ON THE OUTSKIRTS OF THE MAGDALENA RIVER. THE CARIBBEAN COAST STILL SEES MAROON COMMUNITIES LIKE SAN BASILIO DE PALENQUE, WHERE THE CREOLE PALENQUERO LANGUAGE IS SPOKEN.

MAROONS

- **VENEZUELA** - IN BARLOVENTO, MANY FREE AND ESCAPED AFRODESCENDIENTES FOUNDED COMMUNITIES, KNOWN AS CUMBES. ONE OF THE MOST WELL-KNOWN OF THESE SETTLEMENTS IS CURIEPE. ANOTHER CUMBE IS OCOYTA, LED BY ESCAPED AFRICAN GUILLERMO RIBAS. THESE VENEZUELAN MAROONS ALSO TRADED IN COCOA. THE CUMBE OF OCOYTA WAS EVENTUALLY DESTROYED IN 1771.
- **MEXICO** - THE MASCOGOS (NEGROS MASCAGOS) ARE A GROUP OF AFRODESCENDIENTES IN COAHUILA, MEXICO. BASED IN THE TOWN OF EL NACIMIENTO. THE GROUP ARE DESCENDANTS OF BLACK SEMINOLES ESCAPING THE THREAT OF SLAVERY IN THE UNITED STATES. THE MASCOGOS CELEBRATE JUNETEENTH.

MAROONS

Garifuna Women Making Cassava Bread early 1900s

THE GARIFUNA PEOPLE:

- THE GARIFUNA, ALSO KNOWN AS GARINAGU, ARE A PEOPLE WHOSE NAME REFERS TO BOTH THEIR LANGUAGE (GARIFUNA) AND THE PEOPLE (GARINAGU).
- THEY ARE THE DESCENDANTS OF ARAWAK, KALINAGO (ISLAND CARIB), AND AFRO-CARIBBEAN PEOPLE.
- TODAY, GARIFUNA COMMUNITIES CAN BE FOUND IN HONDURAS, THE UNITED STATES, AND BELIZE.
- THE TERM GARIFUNA IS THOUGHT TO HAVE ORIGINATED FROM THE KALINAGO (CARIB) TERMS KARIFUNA AND KALINAGO, WHICH WERE LATER ADOPTED BY THE GARIFUNA.
- THE GARIFUNA WERE HISTORICALLY REFERRED TO BY THE EXONYMS CARIBS, BLACK CARIBS, AND ISLAND CARIBS, WITH EUROPEAN EXPLORERS USING THE TERM BLACK CARIBS AS EARLY AS THE 17TH CENTURY.

DIASPORA

TODAY YOU ARE PART OF THE AFRICAN DIASPORA. DIASPORA IS ORIGINALLY A GREEK WORD THAT MEANS THE SPREADING OF SEEDS. AFRICAN DIASPORA REPRESENTS BOTH THE SPREADING OF BLACK PEOPLE TO ALL CORNERS OF THE EARTH AND OF OUR CONNECTION TO EACH OTHER.

LOOKING AT THE MAP AGAIN YOU WILL SEE THAT THE CARIBBEAN, COLOMBIA, AND BRAZIL ARE ALL PLACES THAT AFRICANS WERE CAPTURED AND TAKEN TO AND LATER DISPERSED FROM THOSE POINTS. **HERE ARE THE TOP 10 COUNTRIES TODAY WITH THE HIGHEST POPULATION OF BLACK PEOPLE**

1. UNITED STATES - 46,936,733
2. BRAZIL - 18,584,218
3. HAITI - 9,925,365
4. FRANCE - 3,000,000-5,000,000
5. COLOMBIA - 4,671,160 (INCLUDING MULTIRACIAL
6. YEMEN - 3,500,000
7. SAUDI ARABIA - 3,370,000
8. UNITED KINGDOM - 3,171,916 (INCLUDING MIXED NATIVE BRITISH AND AFRICAN)
9. JAMAICA - 2,510,000
10. MEXICO - 1,386,556

DID ANYTHING ON THE LIST SURPRISE YOU? WHERE DID YOU THINK THE HIGHEST POPULATION WOULD BE?

LATINEGRA DOES NOT MEAN YOU HAVE TO SPEAK SPANISH OR THAT A PERSON IS MIXED RACE. IT IS IMPORTANT TO KNOW THAT THERE IS A DIFFERENCE BETWEEN RACE NATIONALITY, AND ETHNICITY

IN THE UNITED STATES THERE ARE 5 MAIN RACIAL CATEGORIES:
(1) WHITE, (2) BLACK OR AFRICAN AMERICAN, (3) AMERICAN INDIAN OR ALASKA NATIVE, (4) ASIAN, AND (5) NATIVE HAWAIIAN OR OTHER PACIFIC ISLANDER.

NATIONALITY IS THE STATUS OF BELONGING TO A PARTICULAR NATION. IT COULD EITHER BE THE NATION OF BIRTH, RESIDENCE, OR OF CITIZENSHIP. IF I WAS BORN IN BOLIVIA BUT HAVE CITIZENSHIP IN CANADA - MY NATIONALITY IS CANADIAN.

ALTHOUGH PEOPLE SIMPLIFY THE TERM, ETHNICITY IS A LITTLE MORE COMPLICATED.

IN THE SIMPLIFIED FORM, ETHNICITY COULD REPRESENT ANCESTRAL LAND AND ROOTS. BUT IN THE MORE COMPLEX SENSE, ETHNICITY IS A GROUP OF PEOPLE WHO IDENTIFY WITH EACH OTHER BASED ON:

> PERCEIVED SHARED ATTRIBUTES THAT DISTINGUISH THEM FROM OTHER GROUPS. THOSE ATTRIBUTES CAN INCLUDE A COMMON NATION OF ORIGIN, OR COMMON SETS OF ANCESTRY, TRADITIONS, LANGUAGE, HISTORY, SOCIETY, RELIGION, OR SOCIAL TREATMENT (KANCHAN 2012: 69 - 70)

(CHANDRA, KANCHAN (2012). CONSTRUCTIVIST THEORIES OF ETHNIC POLITICS. OXFORD UNIVERSITY PRESS. PP. 69-70.

THAT MEANS ETHNICITY IS BEYOND GEOGRAPHY. WE ARE A DIASPORA.

DUE TO THE SIMILARITY OF THESE WORDS, IT CAN BE SEEN HOW PEOPLE CONFUSE THE MEANINGS.

A PERSON WHOSE NATIONALITY IS AMERICAN
CAN BE OF BLACK, WHITE, ETC. RACE
AND ETHNICALLY PANAMANIAN.

THAT MEANS A PERSON WHO IS PUERTO RICAN
CAN BE BLACK, WHITE, INDIGENOUS, ASIAN, ETC.
AND OF ANY NATIONALITY

WHAT IS YOUR NATIONALITY _____
WHAT IS YOUR RACE/S _____
WHAT IS YOUR ETHNICITY _____

WHO ARE YOU?

_____

_____

_____

_____

_____

IF NO ONE TOLD YOU HOW TO DESCRIBE YOU, HOW WOULD YOU DESCRIBE YOURSELF?

NEW BEGINNINGS

LISTEN TO THIS SONG OR READ THE WORDS AND TALK ABOUT WHAT YOU THINK IT MEANS.
HOW DO YOU THINK THIS CAN BE USEFUL FOR YOU?

GIVE ME THE STRENGTH, YEAH
TO CHANGE WHAT I CAN CHANGE
GIVE ME THE COURAGE
TO ACCEPT WHAT STAYS THE SAME
GIVE ME THE WISDOM
TO KNOW THE DIFFERENCE
I AM CALLING ON A NEW BEGINNING

SOMETIMES IT'S NOT EASY

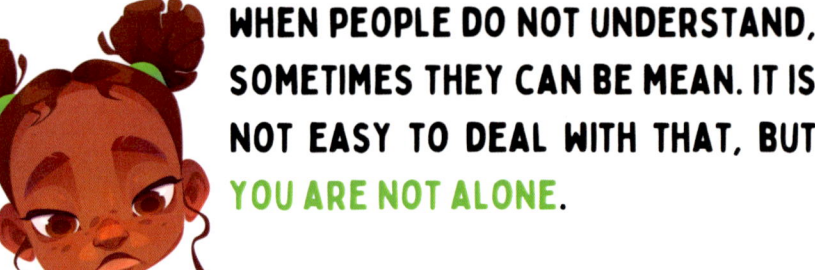

WHEN PEOPLE DO NOT UNDERSTAND, SOMETIMES THEY CAN BE MEAN. IT IS NOT EASY TO DEAL WITH THAT, BUT YOU ARE NOT ALONE.

USE THIS PAGE OF YOUR WORKBOOK TO WRITE THINGS THAT HAVE HAPPENED.

LET'S WRITE

WRITE ABOUT A TIME WHEN YOU FELT REJECTED OR NOT UNDERSTOOD.

WHAT HAPPENED? DO YOU REMEMBER WHEN?

_____
_____
_____
_____

HOW DID IT MAKE YOU FEEL?

_____
_____
_____
_____

WHAT DID YOU DO?

_____
_____
_____
_____

LET'S MAKE IT BETTER!

KNOWLEDGE IS POWER AND NOW THAT YOU KNOW SOME WAYS YOU CAN DEFINE YOURSELF, HOW WOULD YOU HANDLE THE SITUATION DIFFERENTLY?

WE CANNOT STOP PEOPLE FROM BEING MEAN BUT WE CAN ALWAYS CHANGE HOW WE RESPOND. **TIME FOR A QUIZ!**

- WHAT CAN YOU SAY WHEN PEOPLE ASK IF YOU ARE "REALLY" LATINO?

- CAN YOU BE BLACK IF BOTH OF YOUR PARENTS ARE FROM COLOMBIA? WHY?

- IF YOU ARE BORN IN THE UNITED STATES AND DO NOT SPEAK SPANISH, ARE YOU STILL LATINO? WHY?

GOOD JOB!! NOW YOU HAVE WAYS TO RESPOND WHEN PEOPLE ASK YOU UNCOMFORTABLE QUESTIONS OR SAY THINGS THAT MAKE YOU FEEL REJECTED.

DON'T LET ANYBODY TELL YOU HOW YOU SHOULD DEFINE YOURSELF!

WHAT DO YOU LOVE MOST ABOUT YOUR RACE? HOW ABOUT YOUR ETHNICITY? WHAT ABOUT YOUR NATIONALITY?

WHAT MAKES YOU BEAUTIFUL?

1. _____
2. _____
3. _____

WRITE 3 THINGS THAT YOU LOVE ABOUT YOURSELF

DID YOU KNOW?
THERE ARE SO MANY PARTS OF LATINO CULTURE AND LANGUAGE THAT ORIGINATED IN AFRICA? HERE ARE A FEW

WORDS WITH AFRICAN ORIGIN

- **CUMBIA** - FROM THE COLGOLESE WORD, NKUMBI WHICH MEANS DRUM - OR NKÚMBA WHICH IS A DANCE

- **LIMBO** - FROM CONGO

- **MOCHILA** - KIKONGO AND KIMBUNDU WORD (MU) NZILA: MEANS A TYPE OF BAG USED TO CARRY OBJECTS.

- **CHEVERE** - MEANS "COOL": FROM EFIK LANGUAGE CHEVERE, BROUGHT BY THE ABAKUA (ABAKPA REGION IN NIGERIA) IN CUBA

- **ASERE** - ASERE COMES FROM THE WORD ESIERE FROM THE EFIK LANGUAGE, ALSO KNOWN AS IBIBIO-EFIK, MEMBER OF THE BENUE-CONGO FAMILY OF LANGUAGES FROM NIGERIA.

- **ÑAME** - FULANI NYAMI "TO EAT."

- **GANDULES** - PIDGEON PEAS DERIVE FROM KIKONGO "WANDU" (BECOMING WANDULES/ANDULES IN PORTUGUESE) OR FROM KIMBUNDU "OANDA", WHICH IS THEIR NAME FOR THE SAME PLANT

- **CONGA** - FROM CONGO

- **MARIMBA** - BANTU LANGUAGE: REPRESENTED BY KIMBUNDU MARIMBA, FROM THE SAME FAMILY AS CHILUBA MADIMBA MARIMBA.

WORDS WITH AFRICAN ORIGIN

- **MOFONGO** - FROM BANTU MOFONGO, MORE SPECIFICALLY FROM THE ANGOLAN KIKONGO TERM MFWENGE-MFWENGE, WHICH MEANS "A GREAT AMOUNT OF ANYTHING AT ALL".

- **MONDONGO** - KIKONGO LANGUAGE, MEANING "INTESTINES, ENTRAILS OF CERTAIN ANIMALS

- **BANANA** - FROM WOLOF BAANANA

- **JIRAFA** - COMES FROM ARABIC ZARAFA AND THOUGHT TO BE DERIVED FROM AFRICA

- **GATO** - BERBER ORIGIN - CAT

- **CANOE** - FROM MANDINKA CANOA

- **CACHIMBO** - BANTU LANGUAGE, KIMBUNDU WORD "KIXIMBU."

- **YANGA** - THE NAME "YANGA" - GASPAR YANGA WAS A PROMINENT FIGURE IN MEXICAN HISTORY. YANGA LED A REBELLION AGAINST SLAVERY IN THE COLONIAL ERA. THE NAME "YANGA" IS OF AFRICAN ORIGIN AND IS ASSOCIATED WITH THE YORUBA PEOPLE.

- **CUMBÉ** - THE WORD "CUMBÉ" IS COMMONLY USED IN AFRO-LATIN MUSIC AND DANCE, PARTICULARLY IN COLOMBIA. IT FINDS ITS ROOTS IN THE BANTU LANGUAGE, WHERE IT MEANS "DRUM."

- **DENGUE** FEVER - KIKONGO AND KIMBUNDU ORIGIN. IN THIS WAY, IT COULD BE TRANSLATED AS " CHILDISH ANGER ".

WORDS WITH AFRICAN ORIGIN

- **BEMBA** – THICK LIPS – BANTU ORIGIN: THE BEMBA ARE ONE OF THE LARGER ETHNIC GROUPS IN ZAMBIA. THE WORD BEMBA ORIGINALLY MEANT A GREAT EXPANSE LIKE THE SEA.

- **BACHATA** – AFRICAN ORIGIN, ORIGINALLY MEANT A LIVELY PARTY AS OPPOSSED TO A MUSIC GENRE

- **BAQUINÉ** – LITTLE ANGEL'S WAKE

- **BEMBETEO** – A TALKATIVE PERSON, USUALLY SOMEONE WHO SPEAKS WAY MORE THAN THEY THEY SHOULD

- **BOCHINCHE** – GOSSIP

- **CALALÚ** – VEGETABLE LIKE SPINACH: GENERALLY WEST AFRICAN MAY BE FROM BENIN CALULU

- **BAMBI** – BANTU MUBAMBI, ONE WHO LIES DOWN IN ORDER TO HIDE: POSITION OF ANTELOPE FAWN FOR CONCEALMENT (CF. WALT DISNEY, BAMBI).

- **CHANGO** – A TYPE OF BLACK BIRD, MONKEY (MEX.) : DEITY OF LIGHTNING, ORIGIN YORUBA

- **CHECHE** – BOSS, GURU

- **GRIFERÍA** – AFRICAN HAIR

- **GUINGAMBÓ** – OKRA

NICOMEDES SANTA CRUZ
PERU'S LEADING ETHNOMUSICOLOGIST

BIRTHPLACE: LIMA, PERU

BIRTH DATE: JUNE 4, 1925

DIED: FEBRUARY 5, 1992 (AGED 66) MADRID, SPAIN

ETHNICITY: PERUVIAN

PROFESSION: POET, COMPOSER, JOURNALIST, FOLKLORIST

RITMOS NEGROS DEL PERU

RITMOS DE LA ESCLAVITUD
CONTRA AMARGURAS Y PENAS.
AL COMPÁS DE LAS CADENAS
RITMOS NEGROS DEL PERÚ.
DE ÁFRICA LLEGÓ MI ABUELA
VESTIDA CON CARACOLES,
LA TRAJERON LO` EPAÑOLES
EN UN BARCO CARABELA.
LA MARCARON CON CANDELA,
LA CARIMBA FUE SU CRUZ.
Y EN AMÉRICA DEL SUR
AL GOLPE DE SUS DOLORES
DIERON LOS NEGROS TAMBORES
RITMOS DE LA ESCLAVITUD

INTERESTING FACT: NICOMEDES SANTA CRUZ IS FROM LA VICTORIA, A HISTORICALLY BLACK SECTION OF LIMA, PERU.

NICOMEDES SANTA CRUZ GAMARRA WAS KNOWN FOR HIS EXCEPTIONAL SINGING OF DÉCIMAS AND STUDYING DIFFERENT PERUVIAN MUSIC AND DANCES, ESPECIALLY OF THE AFRICAN DIASPORA. HE WAS HIGHLY REGARDED AS PERU'S TOP ETHNOMUSICOLOGIST. SANTA CRUZ DEDICATED HIMSELF TO THE REVIVAL OF AFRO PERUVIAN FOLKLORE, USING HIS THEATER COMPANY, CONJUNTO CUMANANA, WHICH HE CO-FOUNDED WITH HIS SISTER, VICTORIA SANTA CRUZ AS A CATALYST TO BRING LIGHT TO INJUSTICES, RACISM, AND SOCIAL ISSUES ENCOUNTERED BY AFROPERUVIANS. THEY UTILIZED THEIR THEATER COMPANY TO ENCOURAGE YOUNG AFROLATINOS TO DISCOVER THEIR AFROPERUVIAN ROOTS.

ESCRAVA ANASTACIA
FREEDOM FIGHTING SAINT

BIRTHPLACE: WEST AFRICA OR BRAZIL

BIRTH DATE: CIRCA MAY 12, 1740

DIED: UNKNOWN

ETHNICITY: ENSLAVED IN BRAZIL

PROFESSION: VENERATED SAINT

ESCRAVA ANASTACIA CONTINUES TO REPRESENT A SYMBOL OF FREEDOM, RESISTANCE AND COMPASSION

ANASTACIA, A WOMAN SHROUDED IN MYSTERY, HER UNIQUE BACKGROUND HAS BAFFLED MANY. ACCORDING TO SOME ACCOUNTS, SHE WAS BORN IN WEST AFRICA AND WAS A MEMBER OF THE ROYAL GALANGA (BANTU) PEOPLE. ALL THE GALANGAL WERE CAPTURED AND ENSLAVED AND TAKEN TO RIO, BRAZIL. HER MOTHER, DELMINDA WAS ASSAULTED BY A WHITE ENSLAVER AND SOLD WHILE PREGNANT WITH ANASTACIA. ANASTACIA WAS ONE OF THE FIRST ENSLAVED CHILDREN TO BE BORN WITH BLUE EYES AND HER BEAUTY HAS BEEN THE SUBJECT OF MANY LEGENDS. SOME BELIEVE THAT HER BEAUTY WAS THE REASON SHE WAS FORCED TO WEAR THE IRON TORTURE MASK. HOWEVER, PEOPLE FROM MINAS-GERAIS, BRAZIL, HAVE A DIFFERENT STORY ABOUT ANASTACIA. THEY SAY THAT SHE CARRIED THE SECRETS OF THE WHITE ENSLAVERS TO BLACK PEOPLE AND PLOTTED WITH THEM TO REBEL. THEY PLACED AN IRON MUZZLE ON HER TO KEEP HER FROM TALKING, BUT SHE FOUND A WAY TO CONTINUE PLOTTING AND STRATEGIZING, WHISPERING PLANS TO THE PEOPLE THROUGH THE MUZZLE. UNFORTUNATELY, SHE DIED OF TETANUS CAUSED BY THE MUZZLE. BEFORE SHE PASSED, SHE CURED AN ENSLAVER'S CHILD OF A SERIOUS ILLNESS AND FORGAVE THEM FOR THEIR PREVIOUS ILL-TREATMENT OF HER. TODAY, ANASTACIA HAS DEVOTEES ALL OVER THE WORLD, AND THERE IS EVEN A FIGHT TO RECOGNIZE HER AS AN OFFICIAL SAINT OF THE CATHOLIC CHURCH.

ROBERTO CLEMENTE
FIRST PLAYER BORN IN LATIN AMERICA INDUCTED INTO THE BASEBALL HALL OF FAME

BIRTHPLACE: CAROLINA, PUERTO RICO

BIRTH DATE: AUGUST 18, 1934

DIED: DECEMBER 31, 1972 (AGED 38) SAN JUAN, PUERTO RICO

ETHNICITY: PUERTO RICAN

PROFESSION: HUMANITARIAN, PROFESSIONAL BASEBALL PLAYER

BASEBALL HALL OF FAMER ROBERTO ENRIQUE CLEMENTE WALKER BECAME THE FIRST LATIN AMERICAN PLAYER TO COLLECT 3,000 CAREER HITS

AT JUST 18 YEARS OLD, ROBERTO CLEMENTE BEGAN HIS CAREER IN PUERTO RICAN PROFESSIONAL BASEBALL, PLAYING FOR THE SANTURCE CANGREJEROS (CRABBERS). THE BROOKLYN DODGERS OFFERED HIM A CONTRACT WHILE HE WAS PLAYING IN THE PUERTO RICAN LEAGUE. IN 1955 WHEN THE PIRATES HAD THE FIRST PICK OF THE SEASON, CLEMENTE MADE HIS DEBUT WITH THE PIRATES ON APRIL 17, 1955, WEARING THE UNIFORM NUMBER 13. HOWEVER, HE CHANGED TO NUMBER 21 DURING THE FIRST GAME OF A DOUBLEHEADER AGAINST THE BROOKLYN DODGERS.

EARLY ON IN HIS CAREER WITH THE PIRATES, HE ENCOUNTERED RACIAL AND ETHNIC TENSION, HOWEVER, NEAR THE END OF HIS CAREER, CLEMENTE COMMENTED, "MY GREATEST SATISFACTION COMES FROM HELPING TO ERASE THE OLD OPINION ABOUT LATIN AMERICANS AND BLACKS." IN LATE DECEMBER 1972, AFTER A MASSIVE EARTHQUAKE HIT NICARAGUA, CLEMENTE DECIDED TO ACCOMPANY THE SUPPLY PLANE FOR A HUMANITARIAN EFFORT IN NICARAGUA. SHORTLY AFTER TAKEOFF FROM THE SAN JUAN AIRPORT ON DECEMBER 31, 1972, THE PLANE CRASHED, KILLING CLEMENTE.

CELIA CRUZ

BIRTHPLACE: HAVANA, CUBA
BIRTH DATE: OCTOBER 21, 1925
DIED: JULY 19, 2003 (AGED 77) FORT LEE, NEW JERSEY, U.S.
ETHNICITY: CUBAN
PROFESSION: SINGER

DID YOU KNOW THAT IN 1987 CELIA CRUZ PERFORMED A CONCERT IN SANTA CRUZ DE TENERIFE, CANARY ISLANDS THAT WAS RECOGNIZED BY THE GUINNESS BOOK OF WORLD RECORDS AS THE LARGEST FREE-ENTRY OUTDOOR CONCERT, WITH AN AUDIENCE OF 250,000 PEOPLE.

CRUZ'S BIG BREAK CAME IN 1950 WHEN MYRTA SILVA, THE SINGER WITH CUBA'S SONORA MATANCERA, RETURNED TO HER NATIVE PUERTO RICO. SINCE THEY WERE IN NEED OF A NEW SINGER, THE BAND DECIDED TO GIVE THE YOUNG CELIA CRUZ A CHANCE. SHE WAS THE ENSEMBLE'S FIRST BLACK FRONT PERSON SINCE ITS FOUNDING ABOUT 25 YEARS EARLIER. CRUZ DEBUTED WITH THE GROUP IN 1950. IN TOTAL CRUZ RECORDED 188 SONGS WITH THE MATANCERA. CRUZ'S ASSOCIATION WITH THE FANIA LABEL BEGUN IN 1973. CRUZ RECORDED HER FIRST STUDIO ALBUM FOR FANIA IN 1974 IN COLLABORATION WITH JOHNNY PACHECO, THE LABEL'S FOUNDER AND MUSICAL DIRECTOR. SUCCESS CAME AFTER CRUZ BECAME IDENTIFIED WITH SALSA MUSIC AND LATER SHE WAS GIVEN THE MONICKER OF THE HE "QUEEN OF SALSA". HER MANY HONOURS INCLUDE THREE GRAMMY AWARDS AND FOUR LATIN GRAMMYS.

JOSÉ CELSO BARBOSA

BIRTHPLACE: BAYAMON, PUERTO RICO

BIRTH DATE: JULY 27, 1857

DIED: SEPTEMBER 21, 1921 (AGED 64) SAN JUAN, PUERTO RICO

ETHNICITY: PUERTO RICAN

PROFESSION: PHYSICIAN, SOCIOLOGIST, PROFESSOR, & POLITICIAN

IN 1880, CELSO EARNED HIS MEDICAL DEGREE FROM THE UNIVERSITY OF MICHIGAN AND WAS THE VALEDICTORIAN. HE WAS THE INSTITUTION'S FIRST PUERTO RICAN STUDENT AND ONE OF THE FIRST PERSONS OF AFRICAN DESCENT TO EARN A MEDICAL DEGREE IN THE UNITED STATES.

AS A HEALTHCARE AND POLITICAL PIONEER, BARBOSA WAS A PHYSICIAN, WHO PROVIDED MEDICAL CARE ACROSS THE ISLAND. HE EVEN INTRODUCED THE CONCEPT OF EMPLOYERS PAYING FOR THEIR WORKERS' FUTURE HEALTHCARE NEEDS, AN EARLY PRECURSOR TO TODAY'S HEALTH INSURANCE. HE WAS AMONG THE FIRST FIVE PUERTO RICAN LEADERS APPOINTED TO THE EXECUTIVE CABINET IN 1900. KNOWN AS THE "FATHER OF THE PUERTO RICAN STATEHOOD MOVEMENT," BARBOSA FOUNDED THE REPUBLICAN PARTY OF PUERTO RICO IN 1899 AND LAUNCHED EL TIEMPO, THE ISLAND'S FIRST BILINGUAL NEWSPAPER, IN 1907.

SYLVIA DEL VILLARD-MORENO
"LA MAJESTAD NEGRA" (BLACK MAJESTY)

BIRTHPLACE: SAN TURCE, PUERTO RICO

BIRTH DATE: FEBRUARY 28, 1928

DIED: FEBRUARY 28, 1990 IN SAN JUAN PUERTO RICO (AGED 62)

ETHNICITY: PUERTO RICAN

PROFESSION: ACTRESS, DANCER, CHOREOGRAPHER AND AFRO-PUERTO RICAN ACTIVIST

VILLARD-MORENO CAME TO THE UNITED STATES ON A GOVERNMENT SCHOLARSHIP FROM PUERTO RICO TO ATTEND FISK UNIVERSITY, AN

HBCU
(HISTORICALLY BLACK COLLEGE/UNIVERSITY)

SHE WAS A TALENTED ACTRESS, DANCER, CHOREOGRAPHER AND AFROPUERTO RICAN ACTIVIST WHOSE GRACEFUL MOVEMENTS AND POWERFUL PRESENCE EARNED HER THE NAME, "LA MAJESTAD NEGRA". SHE CHERISHED AND CELEBRATED HER BEAUTIFUL AFRICAN ROOTS. AND TRACED HER HERITAGE TO THE YORUBA AND IGBO TRIBES OF NIGERIA. SADLY, THE LOVE OF HER ROOTS CAUSED SOME SUFFERING FOR HER IN PUERTO RICO. WHEN SHE SPOKE OUT AGAINST A POPULAR CHARACTER, CHIANITA THAT WAS PLAYED IN BLACKFACE. THEY BANNED HER FROM TELEVISION AND TRIED TO SHUT DOWN HER THEATERS. STILL, SHE WENT ON TO FOUND MANY IMPORTANT THEATERS SUCH AS TEATRO AFRO-BORICUA EL COQUÍ.

VICENTE GUERRERO
THE FIRST BLACK PRESIDENT OF MEXICO

BIRTHPLACE: TIXTLA, MEXICO

BIRTH DATE: AUGUST 10, 1782

DIED: FEBRUARY 14, 1831 (AGED 48) OAXACA, MEXICO

ETHNICITY: MEXICAN

PROFESSION: MILITARY OFFICER, POLITICIAN

VICENTE RAMÓN GUERRERO SALDAÑA

VICENTE GUERRERO WAS THE FIRST AFRODESCENDIENTE ELECTED AS PRESIDENT OF MEXICO. HE ABOLISHED THE SYSTEM OF CASTES AND A KEY ACHIEVEMENT OF HIS PRESIDENCY WAS THE TOTAL ABOLITION OF SLAVERY IN MEXICO. ADIDITIONALLY, HE SUPPORTED PUBLIC SCHOOLS, LAND TITLE REFORM, AND INDUSTRY DEVELOPMENT.

UNFORTUNATELY, SOON AFTER ABOLISHING SLAVERY, HE WAS BETRAYED BY HIS VICE PRESIDENT. THEY INVITED HIM TO A DINNER AND OVERTHREW HIM FROM OFFICE VIA REBELLION. ON FEBRUARY 14, 1831, HE WAS EXECUTED BY FIRING SQUAD.

MANY HISTORIANS DEBATE OVER WHY THEY KILLED HIM AS OPPOSED TO SENDING HIM INTO EXILE. SOME ARGUE THAT IT IS BECAUSE OF HIS RACE AND BECAUSE OF THE SUCCESSFUL ABOLITION OF ENSLAVEMENT.

ARTURO SCHOMBURG

BIRTHPLACE: SAN TURCE, PUERTO RICO

BIRTH DATE: JANUARY 24, 1874

DIED: JUNE 10, 1938 (AGED 64) BROOKLYN, NEW YORK, U.S.

ETHNICITY: PUERTO RICAN

PROFESSION: AUTHOR, HISTORIAN, WRITER, COLLECTOR, AND ACTIVIST

WHILE SCHOMBURG WAS IN GRADE SCHOOL, ONE OF HIS TEACHERS CLAIMED THAT BLACK PEOPLE HAD NO HISTORY

IN 1896, SCHOMBURG BEGAN TEACHING SPANISH IN NEW YORK. SOON, HE GAINED ATTENTION FOR HIS WRITING, WITH HIS FIRST KNOWN ARTICLE, "IS HAYTI DECADENT?" (1904). IN 1911, SCHOMBURG CO-FOUNDED THE SOCIETY FOR HISTORICAL RESEARCH, UNITING SCHOLARS FROM THROUGHOUT THE AFRICAN DIASPORA FOR THE FIRST TIME. SCHOMBURG HAD AN EXTENSIVE COLLECTION OF ARTWORKS, MANUSCRIPTS, RARE BOOKS, AND OTHER ARTIFACTS RELATING TO THE AFRICAN DIASPORA. THIS COLLECTION BECAME THE SCHOMBURG CENTER FOR RESEARCH IN BLACK CULTURE.

AFROLATINO HISTORY

IMAGINE HOW MANY AMAZING ACCOMPLISHMENTS HAVE BEEN MADE BY AFROLATINOS YOU CAN ALSO MAKE HISTORY. WHAT DO YOU WANT TO BE WHEN YOU GROW UP?

1. _____
2. _____
3. _____

YANZA
WINDS OF CHANGE
OMILANI - FROM ALBUM ORE YEYE O

ANCIENT WINDS
BLOWING FROM AFRICA
CARRYING THE VOICES
OF OUR ANCESTORS
BREEZING
OVER LAND AND SEA
WHIRLING HIGH ABOVE
A CYCLONE ENCIRCLING ME:

A SKIRT
DRAPING LIKE COLORFUL BLADES
A NAT TURNER REBELLION
FREEING THE SLAVES
YOU KNOW THAT CHILL
THAT YOU FEEL IN THE WIND:

SOME THINGS HAVE TO BE LET GO
SO YOU CAN BEGIN AGAIN
SOME THINGS HAVE TO BE LET GO
SO YOU CAN BEGIN
AGAIN.

DO NOT LET ANYONE TELL YOU THAT YOU DO NOT HAVE A CULTURE

INNOVATORS   CREATORS   ORIGINATORS   CELEBRATORS

People of the African diaspora have influenced many aspects of society, including food, language, and clothing styles. Despite originating and laying the foundations for much of mainstream society, they have also been punished and made to feel ashamed for their contributions and style.

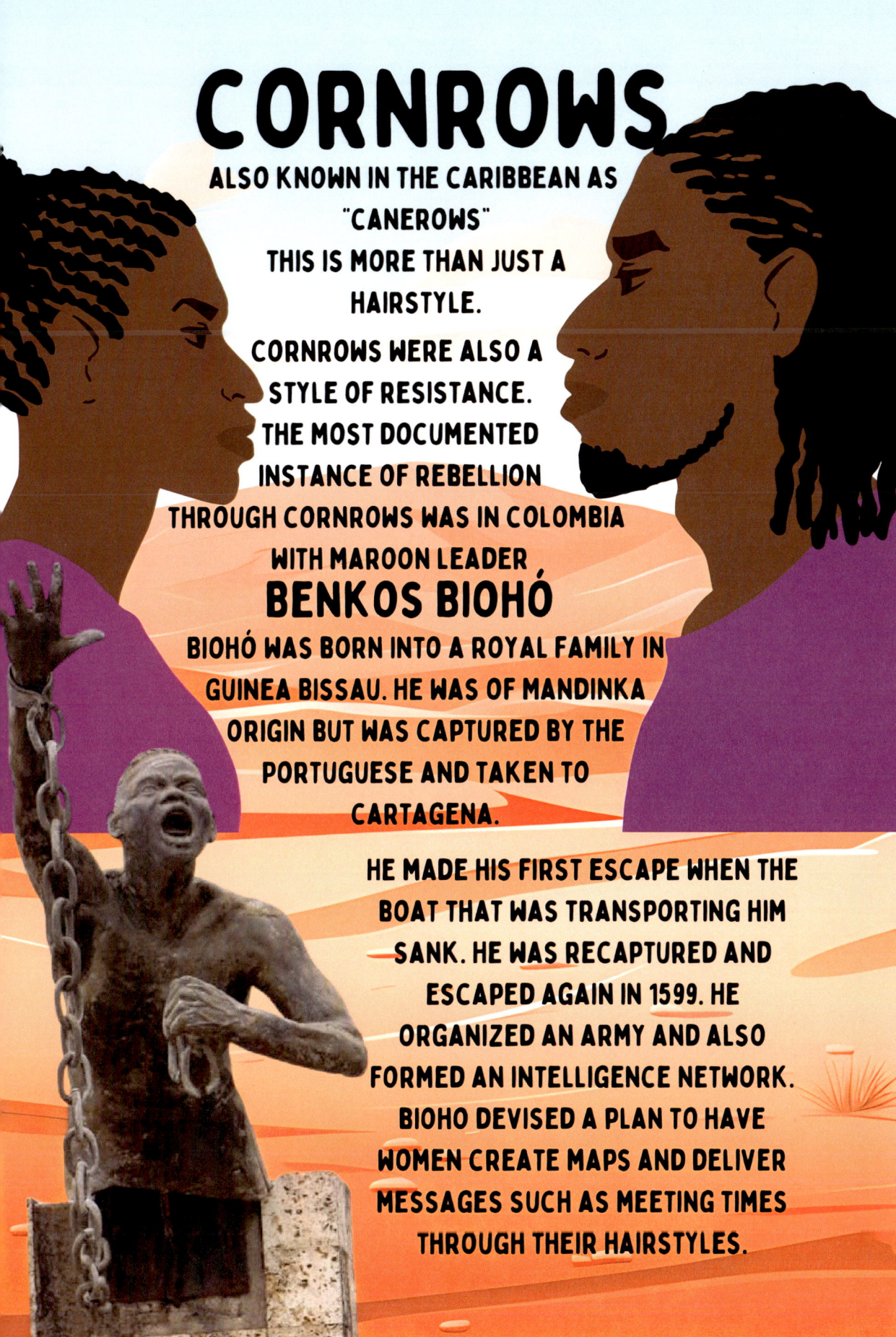

RELIGIOUS FREEDOM

MANY OF US WERE TAUGHT IN SCHOOL THAT ONE OF THE PRIMARY REASONS EUROPEANS CAME TO THE NEW WORLD WAS TO ESCAPE RELIGIOUS PERSECUTION. IRONICALLY, THE SAME PEOPLE WHO FLED PERSECUTION, OPPRESSED AFRICAN TRADITIONAL PRACTICES AND TAUGHT THEM THAT ANYTHING FROM THEIR HOMELAND WAS EVIL AND DIABOLICAL. YET MANY OF THE AFRICAN TRADITIONAL PRACTICES SURVIVED, ADAPTED, AND CONTINUE TO THRIVE TODAY. THE STIGMA AND PERCEPTION OF THE PRACTICES AS EVIL AND "UNGODLY" PERSISTS, YET THERE IS A CONTINUOUS EFFORT TO BROADEN THE HORIZON OF UNDERSTANDING AND RE-EDUCATE PEOPLE ABOUT AFRICAN CULTURAL AND TRADITIONAL PRACTICES.

SOME OF THE LARGEST SURVIVING COMMUNITIES ARE DESCENDED FROM THE YORUBA SUCH AS: SANTERIA (CUBA), CANDOMBLE (BRAZIL), AND SHANGO BAPTIST (TRINIDAD & TOBAGO) AND KIKONGO TRADITIONS THAT SURVIVED ARE: UMBANDA, VOUDOU, PALO MAYOMBE, AND ABAKUA.

THIS IS DUE, IN PART, TO THE FACT THAT ENTIRE KINGDOMS WERE CAPTURED RELATIVELY LATE IN THE TRANS-ATLANTIC SLAVE TRADE AND RETAINED MANY OF THE CUSTOMS AND TRADITIONS.

TIGNON LAWS

"......the alluvion of the free negro and quadroon women is very detrimental, and those who abandon themselves to same, is because they subsist from the product of their licentious life without abstaining from carnal pleasures, for which I admonish them to drop all communication and intercourse of vice, and go back to work, with the understanding that I will be suspicious of their indecent conduct, by the extravagant luxury in their dressing which already is excessive, and this only circumstance will compel me to investigate the customs of those who will present themselves in this manner. The distinction which exists in the hair dressing of the colored people, from the others, is necessary for same to subsist, and order the quadroon and negro women, wear feathers, nor curls in their hair, combing same flat or covering it with a handkerchief if it is combed high as was formerly the custom."

PAINTING: "PORTRAIT OF A YOUNG WOMAN" JEAN-ETIENNE LIOTARD - LATE 18TH CENTURY)

IN 1786, THE SPANISH GOVERNOR OF LOUISIANA, ESTEBAN RODRIGUEZ MIRÓ, PASSED THE TIGNON LAW (ALSO KNOWN AS THE CHIGNON LAW) TO ADDRESS CONCERNS THAT WOMEN OF AFRICAN DESCENT WERE DRESSING IN A FASHIONABLE AND WEALTHY MANNER, WHICH THREATENED THE STATUS QUO AND MADE WHITE WOMEN FEEL INSECURE. AS A RESULT, BLACK, CREOLE AND MULATA WOMEN WERE REQUIRED TO WEAR A HEADWRAP CALLED A TIGNON, WHICH COVERED THEIR HAIR, AND WERE PROHIBITED FROM WEARING FEATHERS AND JEWELS. HOWEVER, THE AFRO-DESCENDANT WOMEN ADAPTED THEIR SENSE OF STYLE TO THIS LAW AND WORE VERY ELABORATE HEADWRAPS MADE OF EXPENSIVE MATERIALS. EVEN AFTER THE LOUISIANA PURCHASE OF 1803, SOME WOMEN CONTINUED TO WEAR HEADWRAPS AS A FORM OF RESISTANCE AGAINST COLONIALISM.

"PAINTING: CREOLE IN A RED TURBAN" JGL AMONS (CIRCA 1840)

WE HAVE WEATHERED THE STORM

The road has not been easy, but through it all, we are still here! More than that, we continue to create and reinvent ourselves. If anything, becoming a diaspora has given us the strength to draw upon the best of all that we are through time and history. The journey hasn't been smooth, but we persevere with the strength of our rich heritage, culture, and history.

> "...facing the rising sun
> of our new day begun
> let us march on
> 'til victory is won"
>
> **James Weldon Johnson**
> *"Lift Ev'ry Voice" (Black National Anthem)*

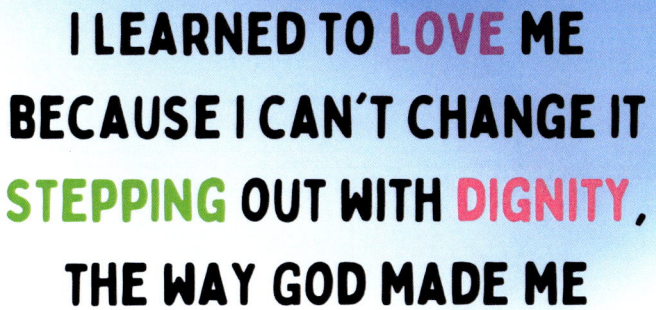

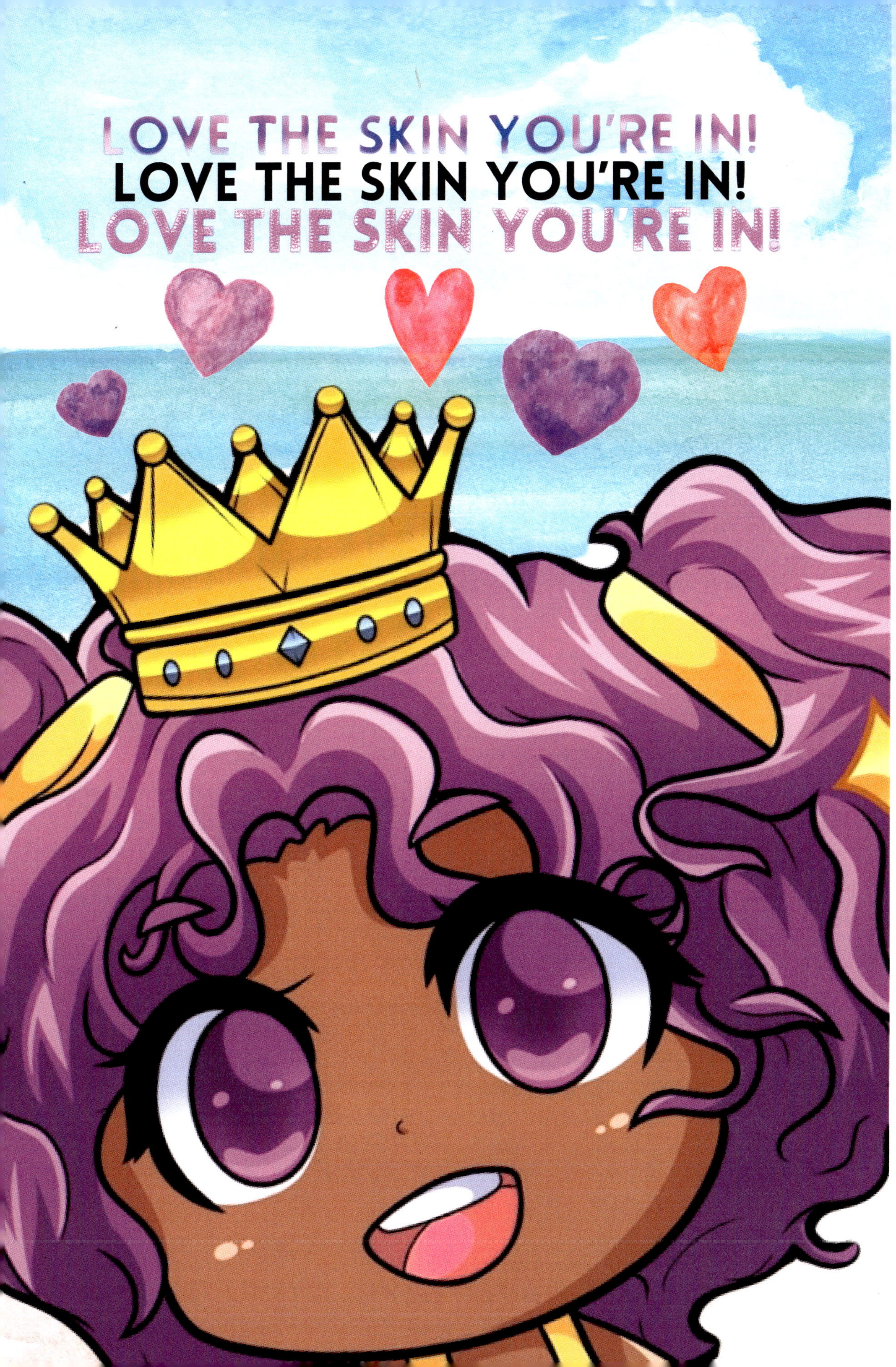
LOVE THE SKIN YOU'RE IN!
LOVE THE SKIN YOU'RE IN!
LOVE THE SKIN YOU'RE IN!

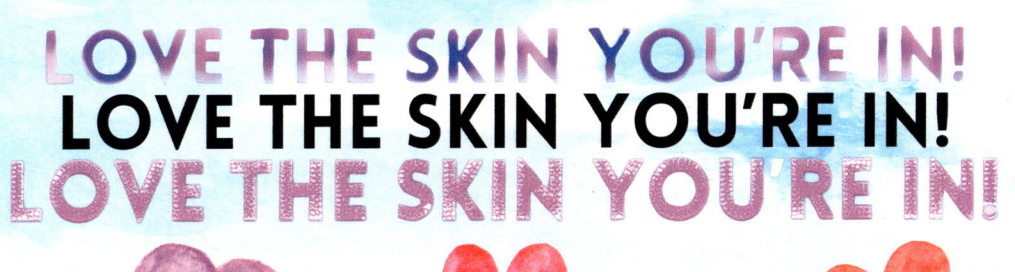

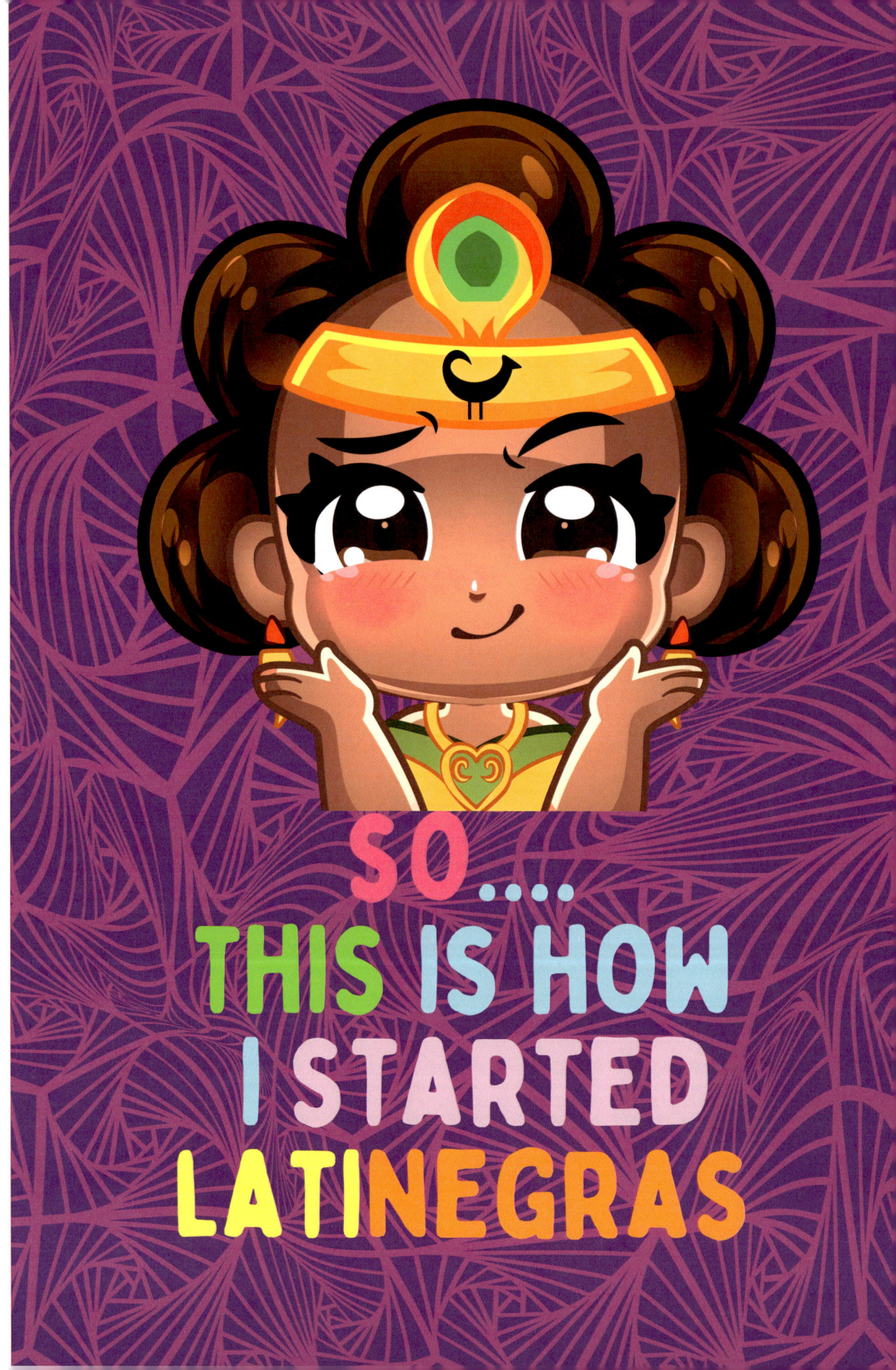

A STUDENT SHARED WITH ME THE STORY OF HOW THEIR PARENTS TOLD THEM TO NEVER BRING HOME ANY DARK-SKINNED BOY. AT THAT MOMENT, I KNEW I HAD TO DO SOMETHING.

I WROTE A SONG (LATINEGRAS) AND BROUGHT IT TO SCHOOL THE NEXT DAY. THE STUDENT RESTED THEIR HEAD ON MY DESK THEY PUT ON THE HEADPHONES AND PLAYED THE SONG OVER AND OVER AND OVER.

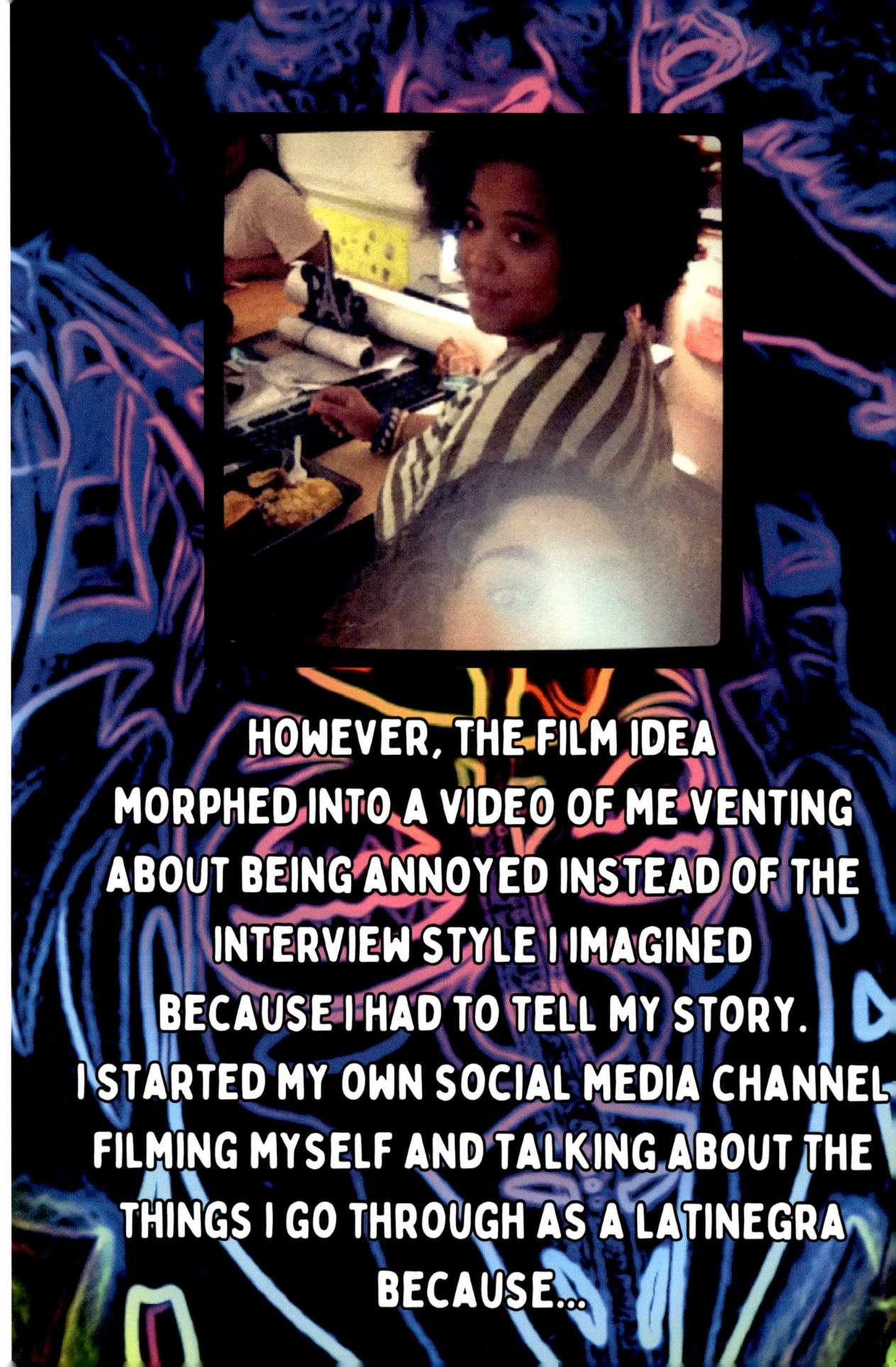

HOWEVER, THE FILM IDEA MORPHED INTO A VIDEO OF ME VENTING ABOUT BEING ANNOYED INSTEAD OF THE INTERVIEW STYLE I IMAGINED BECAUSE I HAD TO TELL MY STORY. I STARTED MY OWN SOCIAL MEDIA CHANNEL FILMING MYSELF AND TALKING ABOUT THE THINGS I GO THROUGH AS A LATINEGRA BECAUSE...

THROUGH PARTICIPATING AS A PERFORMING ARTIST IN THE SPOKEN SOUL FESTIVAL – AN ANNUAL ARTS FESTIVAL THAT CELEBRATES WOMEN ARTISTS – I HAD THE CHANCE TO CONNECT WITH ITS FOUNDER, DEBORAH MAGDALENA. AFTER AN EVENT, WE HAD A DISCUSSION THAT GAVE ME THE COURAGE TO SPEAK MY TRUTH AND GO ON A MISSION TO COMPLETE THE FILM.

ONCE I TOLD MY TRUTH, PEOPLE NATURALLY APPEARED TO INTERVIEW WITH LATINEGRAS. THE NEXT PICTURES ARE FROM MY FIRST (PRE)SCREENING. THIS WAS SO VALUABLE BECAUSE EVERYONE'S FEEDBACK HELPED ME TO IMPROVE THE FILM.

THE FOLLOWING PICTURES ARE FROM ONE OF THE FIRST SCREENINGS OF LATINEGRAS:

Latinegras: Love the Skin You're In

LATINEGRAS are women of African Descent with roots in Latin America. The term is a combination of two words Latina and Negra.
Did you always love yourself? In a performance style documentary Director/Founder/Filmmaker, Omilani Alarcon combines the arts, music, and reflective voice-overs as echoes of the journey to seek one's inner "beautiful". Notions of beauty and identity are challenged as the question of "who I am" is re-defined through the lens of a multi-generational cast of AfroLatina women. You will find yourself laughing, crying, and enlightened by the roller coaster of thought provoking yet delightful accounts of what it was like growing up Black and Latina. This is a story that relates to anyone who has ever wondered who they are.

THE WOMEN OF LATINEGRAS WERE MORE THAN JUST A CAST. THEY WERE A SISTERHOOD AND A SUPPORT SYSTEM. FOR ME AS A YOUNG FILMMAKER, THEY ENCOURAGED ME TO USE MY VOICE AND TO NOT BE AFRAID OF CHALLENGING MYSELF TO BREAK BARRIERS.

I FEEL LIKE THE RIGHT PEOPLE CAME TOGETHER AT THE RIGHT TIME TO MAKE THE FILM AND WE CONTINUE TO SUPPORT EACH OTHER. LATINEGRAS WAS BEAUTIFUL BOTH ON AND OFF SCREEN.

LATINEGRAS WAS MORE THAN JUST A CAST

MAIN CAST MEMBERS

THESE ARE THE AMAZING WOMEN WHO MADE LATINEGRAS SUCH A BEAUTIFUL PROJECT. THEY ATTENDED SO MANY SCREENINGS, PANEL DISCUSSIONS AND ALWAYS HAVE BEEN SO SUPPORTIVE EVEN AFTER THE PROJECT WAS COMPLETE.

DEBORAH MAGDALENA

YVONNE & YVETTE RODRIGUEZ

OLIVIA BENSON

ISIADA ORTIZ

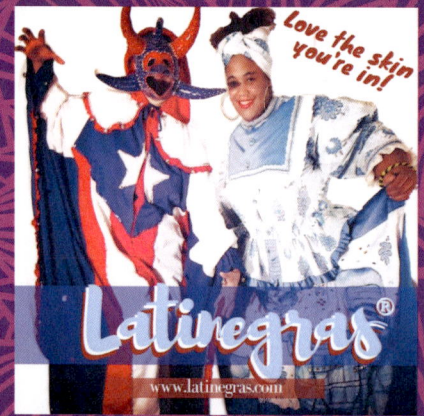

NIKI LOPEZ & NOEL (MOM)

MIAMI FILM FESTIVAL

IT IS STILL SURREAL THAT LATINEGRAS DEBUTED IN REGAL CINEMAS, IN THE SAME CORRIDOR WHERE BLACK PANTHER WAS SCREENING. IT WAS SUCH A BEAUTIFUL FEELING TO SEE ALL THE CAST MEMBERS WALK THE RED CARPET AND TAKE THEIR PHOTOS. IT FELT LIKE WE WERE CELEBRATING FOR ALL OF US!

WE WERE ALSO FEATURED IN THE HOLLYWOOD REPORTER AND NOMINATED FOR THE INAUGURAL KNIGHT MADE IN MIA AWARD.

TO BE ABLE TO SHARE THIS MOMENT AND MANY MORE TO FOLLOW IS THE BEST FEELING IN THE WORLD.

THERE ARE SO MANY PEOPLE TO THANK FOR THIS OPPORTUNITY.

I ATTENDED A WORKSHOP WITH **SUNDANCE** INSTITUTE AND MET THE THE FORMER DIRECTOR OF MIAMI FILM FESTIVAL, **JAIE LAPLANTE**. HE WAS SO AMAZINGLY **ENCOURAGING**.

AT THE TIME I HAD A LOT OF SELF-DOUBT AS A FILMMAKER, BUT I SUBMITTED MY FILM ANYWAY AND THE RESULT WAS FAR MORE THAN WHAT I EVER EXPECTED.

IF I COULD GIVE A **MESSAGE TO YOUNG FILMMAKERS**, IT WOULD BE TO NEVER DOUBT WHAT YOU ARE CAPABLE OF ACCOMPLISHING BECAUSE YOU NEVER KNOW. YOU HAVE TO STEP PAST THE FEAR OR THE FEELING THAT WHAT YOU DO/ARE/HAVE IS NOT GOOD ENOUGH. YOU ARE **ALWAYS ENOUGH**.

BELatina

BELATINA TV | ENTERTAINMENT | NEWS | OUR CULTURA | MODA & BEA

Latinegras: A Miami Film Festival selection about Afro-Latinas and identity

Gomez - August 23, 2019

Share

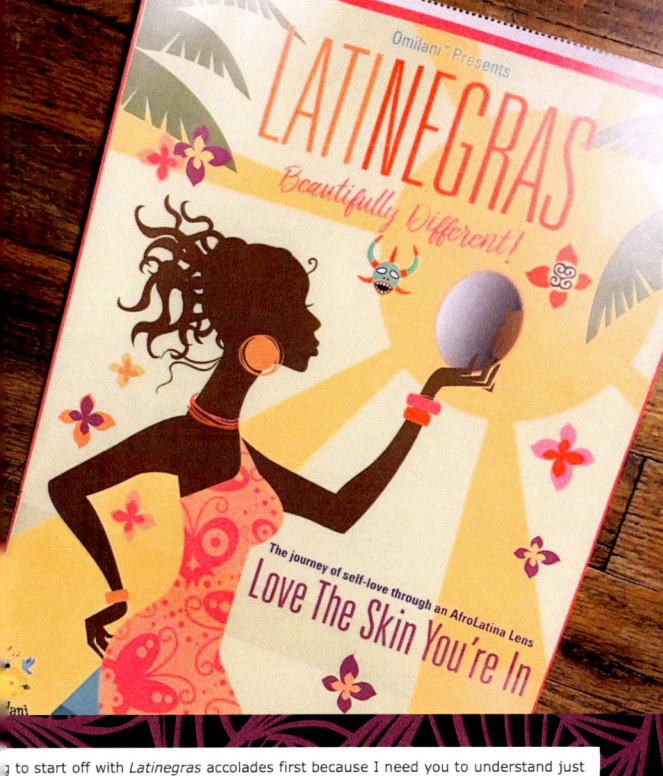

to start off with *Latinegras* accolades first because I need you to understand just this film is before I dig deeper into it. *Latinegras* has recently been chosen as an election of the Miami Film Festival. This is not the only recognition Omilani , *Latinegras* film director and founder, creation acquired. She's also been awarded ctor (Documentary) in Newark International Film Festival, winner of the Afrolatino Award, and a finalist in the Knight Made in MIA Award. As you can tell, this is no film.

Latinegras started with a melodic song that seduced me to watch the ima song that was composed by Omilani Alarcón, who's also a singer and song film predominantly takes place in Miami and Puerto Rico, which are some where pieces of my heart resides.

The documentary started out with a thought-provoking voice over narrate which continued on for the rest of the film. It immediately touched base u people of color in our community. As the film progressed, Omilani remind that once swept the beautiful waters of Puerto Rico. She revived the storie people who died during their voyage to the island because somebody had mandated them to be slaves and how that's also part of many afro-latinas film, Omilani exposes the challenges afro-latinas have to endure living bot Caribbean and in the United States.

The film director placed enough emphasis on *Latinegras* to raise awarenes importance of all identities within the latinx community. She didn't expect be inclusive to the afro-latina community. Instead, she hoped everyone w understand the significance of identities, that way everyone could be educ

This documentary also can be used to help anyone who's ever struggled wi Regardless of race. Her goal was to represent the misrepresented and to u identities, despite the discriminatory stories we may have grown up with.

Photo Credit @treslindascubanascigars

Omilani Alarcón was able to capture the history of Afro-latinas and their id series of mini-interviews with multi-generational latinas she knew. The Cub entrepreneurs, Yvette and Yvonne Rodriguez, were among the cast membe the film. They spoke about how they felt beautiful in their skin, regardless anyone might think of them.

In fact, this was one of the recurring themes of the film — to feel beautiful Omilani made it clear that it was necessary for everyone to understand.

"Accept yourselves and love the skin you're in," this was something Omilan once I asked her about the theme of the film.

Latinegras is currently on the Film Festival circuit and will be screened in ot Omilani also said that the film will be touring the United States, so stay vig screening near your town.

I know I'm not Rotten Tomatoes, but I can give her some Sweet Mangos. I would be the latinx equivalent of Rotten Tomatoes. In any case, this film is Mangos, meaning completely recommendable! I promise you that it is an e need. You will probably be on an emotional rollercoaster, but that's okay. S heart broke to pieces in some moments of the film, while I laughed during You won't regret watching it.

WHAT DID YOU LEARN?

OMILANI ALMOST DIDN'T RELEASE THE LATINEGRAS FILM BECAUSE OF SELF-DOUBT.

LIST 3 WAYS YOU CAN CONQUER YOUR FEARS

1. _____
2. _____
3. _____

The Miami Times

Volume 99 Number 35 | APRIL 13-19, 2022 | MiamiTimesOnline.com | Ninety-Three Cents

A journey toward joy
Spoken Soul celebrates women in the arts

SAMANTHA MORELL
Miami Times Staff Writer

After what they consider to be an especially rough two years – with a pandemic and a crescendo of racial dismay to blame – the women of Spoken Soul just want to have fun, and that's exactly what they did during their annual showcase this month.

The women-centric spoken-word festival celebrated its 14th year April 8 at the Adrienne Arsht Center for the Performing Arts, which has served as a venue for its past five installments. Following a COVID-induced postponement of its 2020 iteration and the decision to forgo the annual showing altogether last year, founding member and director Deborah Magdalena knew just what the Spoken Soul gang needed: to let go of some stress and get back to creating.

That's why she chose to revolve this year's performances around the theme of joy. Following four stages of happiness – what Magdalena refers to as reverse mourning, serving as an antithesis to the five stages of grief – "Girls Just Wanna Have Fun" was all about finding one's inner child. Present to help facilitate that journey was Spoken Soul alumni Mori Taiye, whose narration guided the audience across the individual chapters: Anticipate, Savor, Express and Reflect.

Alumni Mori Taiye narrated the 2022 Spoken Soul showcase with a four-part spoken-word piece.

"[My piece is] bringing all of the emotions and elements of all the pieces together," Taiye said. "I'm kind of like the reminder."

It is through the bad times, Taiye's words reflect, that that reminder is needed most. It's for this reason that she began the program by expressing anger toward the wrongful deaths of Breonna Taylor and George Floyd. It's why Reshma Anwar and Briana Mendez performed a somber dance to artist Annette Gonzalez Silvera's recorded monologue on the heavy weight of motherhood. It's what made Amy Baez's ode to her late father – complemented by Lola Ramirez on the flute and Yarelis Gandul on the drums – fitting for this year's theme, challenging the notion of death as a joyless subject, if not one to be avoided completely.

The one-time performance served as a call to reclaim the spaces where the falsity of perfection demands to be realized and where violence often persists. In that sense, the journey toward happiness is as much a fight as it is a feeling. But once Afro-Filipina musical artist OMILANI hit the stage, the audience knew for certain that this was a time to rejoice.

CELEBRATING ONE'S ROOTS

Presenting for the third time with Spoken Soul, OMILANI brought to the audience a music video for a song from her upcoming album, "Oreyeyo," in order to fulfill her role as the third stage of happiness, Express. The content of the video serves as a play on Canboulay, a portion of Carnival that is celebrated in Trinidad and Tobago, where OMILANI lived for three years and where her career in music b

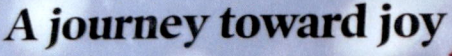

OMILANI shows ... in accordance ... year's Spoken S... Find your inner c...

SAMANTHA MORELL FOR THE MIAMI TIMES (2)

SISTERHOOD IS AMAZING!

LOVING YOURSELF IS GREAT! BUT IMAGINE SHARING THE LOVE WITH SO MANY WONDERFUL PEOPLE

1. WHAT IS YOUR FAVORITE WAY TO SHOW LOVE?

2. HOW CAN YOU SHARE THAT LOVE WITH OTHERS?

3. WHAT IF THEY DO NOT UNDERSTAND YOUR WAY OF SHOWING LOVE?

4. LOVING YOURSELF WILL MAKE YOUR LIFE EASY?

WHAT DID YOU LEARN?

**IN THIS BOOK WE DISCUSSED:
HISTORY, CULTURE, RACE & IDENTITY.
WE ALSO LOOKED AT: THE ANCESTOR'S GREATNESS
& STRUGGLES FOR FREEDOM.**

1. WHAT PART OF THE BOOK DID YOU CONNECT WITH THE MOST?

2. DID ANYTHING SURPRISE YOU?

3. HOW IS THIS INFORMATION HELPFUL IN YOUR DAILY LIFE?

MEANING BEHIND LATINEGRAS LOGO

- **SANKOFA - FROM THE AKAN PEOPLE OF GHANA**

"SE WO WERE FI NA WOSANKOFA A YENKYI"
TWI/GHANAIAN PROVERB (IT IS NOT WRONG TO GO BACK FOR THAT WHICH YOU HAVE FORGOTTEN)

SANKOFA IS A BIRD THAT FLIES FORWARD BY LOOKING BACK INTO THE PAST TO RETRIEVE WHAT IS ESSENTIAL.

SOMETIMES SANKOFA IS REPRESENTED BY THE ADINKRA SYMBOL THAT RESEMBLES A HEART. INTERESTINGLY, THIS SYMBOL CAN ALSO BE FOUND IN THE U.S. ON IRON WORK. SOME HAVE THEORIZED IT WAS CARRIED OVER FROM AFRICA.

THE SANKOFA SYMBOL IS BOTH IN THE HEADBAND AND WORN AROUND THE NECK OF LATINEGRA. THIS IS BECAUSE A BIG PART OF LATINEGRAS IS REACHING BACK INTO HISTORY AND EMBRACING THE CULTURE WE HAVE COME FROM TO LOVE WHO WE ARE.

ATABEY
- ## TAINO ANCESTRAL MOTHER EARTH

LATINEGRAS FOUNDER IN UTUADO, PUERTO RICO AT THE CAGUANA INDIGENOUS CEREMONIAL PARK - THE PETROGLYPH OF ATABEY PICTURED ON LEFT

ATABEY ALSO REPRESENTS WATER. IN THE CONTEXT OF LATINEGRAS, ATABEY REPRESENTS THE DIVINE FEMININE ENERGY, THE ANCESTORS, AND THE WATERS THAT CONNECT ALL PEOPLE OF THE AFRICAN DIASPORA. IT ALSO PAYS TRIBUTE TO INDIGENOUS ROOTS AND THE INTERSECTION OF OUR COMMUNITIES.

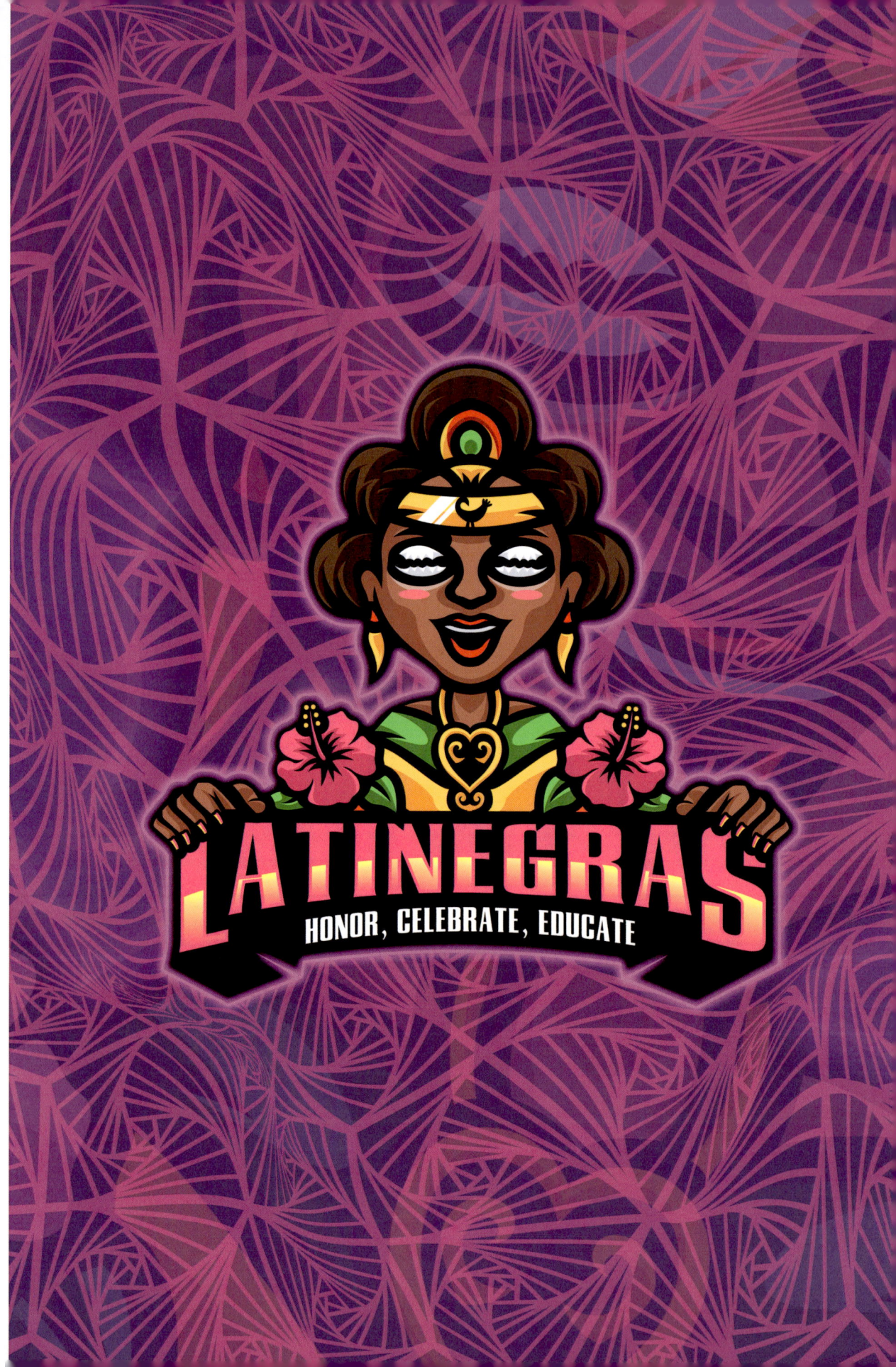

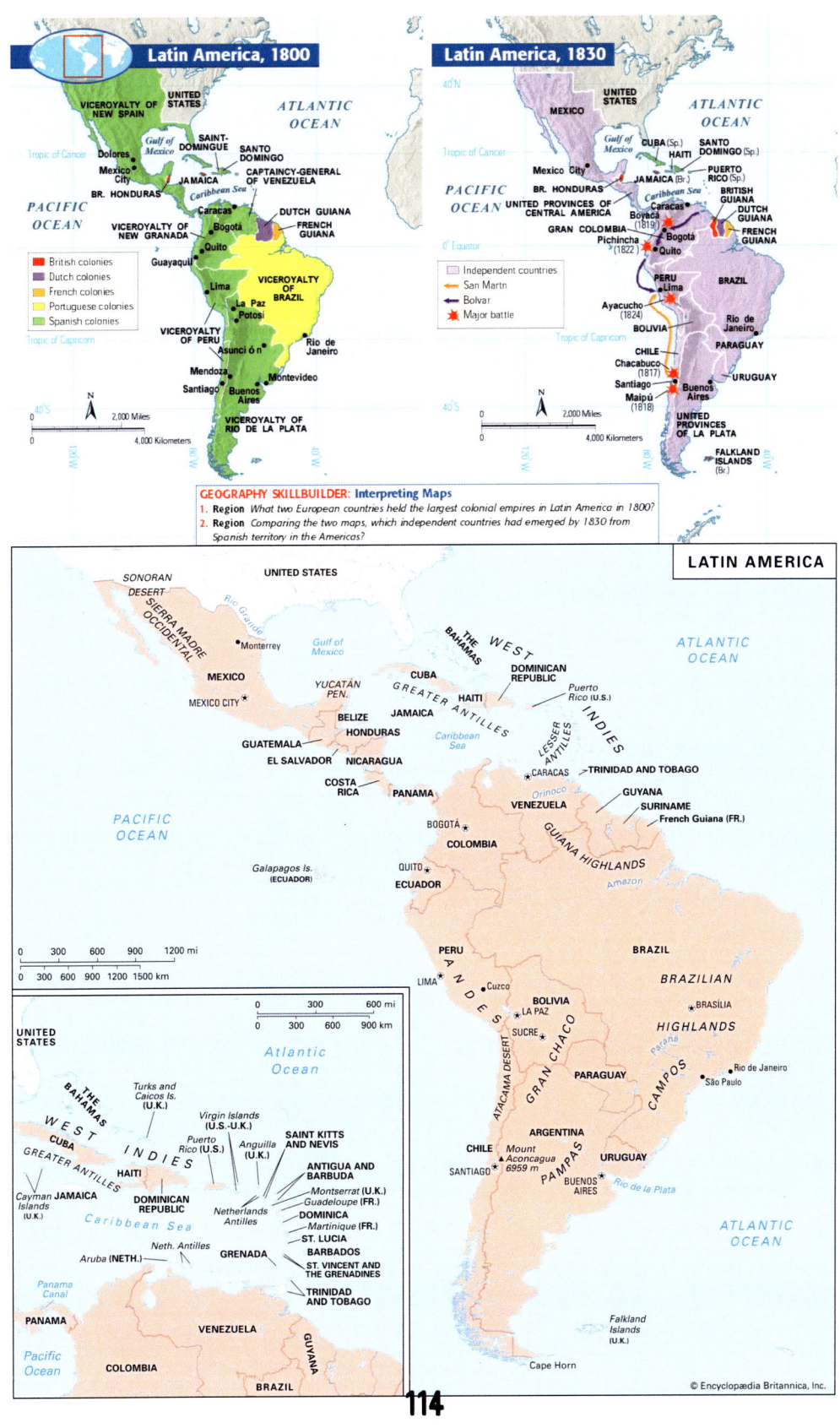

OMILANI ALARCON
LATINEGRAS FOUNDER BIO

OMILANI ALARCON IS A GRADUATE OF CORNELL UNIVERSITY IN ITHACA, NY. SHE GRADUATED SUMMA-CUM-LAUDE AND UPON GRADUATION, IMMEDIATELY EMBARKED UPON A FULBRIGHT-HAYS GPA FELLOWSHIP. SHE COMPLETED A STUDY AT THE UNIVERSITY OF CAMBRIDGE (UK) IN CLASSICAL ART & ARCHITECTURE AS WELL AS RETURNED TO AFRICA, FRANCE, AND THE CARIBBEAN FOR FURTHER RESEARCH.

MS. ALARCÓN IS A VISUAL & PERFORMING ARTIST, POET, SCHOLAR, AND FOUNDER OF THE LATINEGRAS AND AFROFILIPINA BRANDS. SHE HAS OVER 11 SCHOLARLY PUBLICATIONS, 10 ALBUMS, & WAS IN THE TOP 7 GRAMMY SHOWCASE FINALISTS. HER DOCUMENTARY, "LATINEGRAS: THE JOURNEY OF SELF LOVE THROUGH AN AFROLATINA LENS" DEBUTED IN SEVILLE, SPAIN. SHE WON BEST DIRECTOR & HAS ACQUIRED NUMEROUS NOMINATIONS AND AWARDS.

OMILANI MADE HISTORY BY WRITING THE FIRST AFROFILIPINO HISTORY BOOK - DOCUMENTING BLACK-FILIPINO IDENTITY IN THE PHILIPPINES AND THE PHILIPPINE DIASPORA. SHE ALSO WROTE THE FIRST AFROFILIPINO COMIC BOOK SERIES WRITTEN BY AN AFROFILIPINA. SHE CONTINUES TO WORK AS AN INDEPENDENT SCHOLAR, INTERNATIONAL PERFORMING ARTIST, ADVOCACY MODEL/PHILANTHROPIST AND AS AN EDUCATOR TEACHING FRENCH LANGUAGE & LITERATURE.

INAGURAL ISSUE
LATINEGRAS COMIC BOOK ALSO AVAILABLE NOW!!!
THE AMAZING ADVENTURES OF LATINEGRA

www.ingramcontent.com/pod-product-compliance
Lightning Source LLC
Chambersburg PA
CBRC101455010526
44110CB00066B/188